A GARDENER'S GUIDE TO

Vegetables

Editor John Negus

Series Editor Graham Strong

MEREHURST

Merehurst Ltd, Ferry House, 51-57 Lacy Road, Putney, London SW15 1PR

CONTENTS

KEY TO AT A GLANCE TABLES

SOWING/PLANTING   HARVESTING

At a glance tables are your quick guide.
For full information, consult the accompanying text.

*LEFT: The vegetable garden need not be relaxed and casual. It can be
more structured and formal as in this charming traditional garden.*

GROWING
VEGETABLES

Pots, tubs and even the tiniest space in your garden will yield a cornucopia of choice vegetables once you know how easy it is to grow them.

Cultivating, harvesting, preparing and eating food from your garden is all part of the same wonderfully rewarding experience. It should be a grand celebration from garden to table. Our purpose here is to show how simple it is to achieve this goal. Indisputably, home-grown crops have the edge on shop bought. They are particularly enjoyable, tasty and vitamin rich when gathered dew fresh from the garden and prepared within minutes for eating.

ABOVE: *This chocolate brown capsicum has a similar flavour to the red and green varieties and looks spectacular in salads.*

LEFT: *Quiet harmony: A pleasing combination of vegetables and flowers romping on fertile soil in full sun.*

HELP TO ENSURE that your crops are pest and disease free by planning them carefully, and never planting the same crop on the same ground for more than one year in three.

THE VERSATILE VEGETABLE

What is a vegetable? For all intents and purposes it is the edible part of any herbaceous plant, so includes all parts of it – such as roots, bulbs, tubers, stems, leaves, flowers, as well as seeds and fruits.

Without getting too technical, fruits used as vegetables include tomato, capsicum, aubergine, cucumber, melon, vegetable marrow and pumpkin. Stems or shoots include celery, asparagus, leeks and rhubarb. Among leafy vegetables, eaten raw or cooked, are cabbage, Swiss chard, spinach, lettuce, endive and Brussels sprouts.

We eat roots of carrot, parsnip, beetroot, swede and turnip, onion bulbs and potato tubers. Seeds are eaten as vegetables in the mature or immature state. These include green peas, mange-tout, sugar snap peas, sweet corn and broad beans. Flowers known as vegetables include cauliflower, globe artichoke and broccoli.

PREPARING A VEGETABLE PLOT

Vegetable gardens may be of any shape or size, but regardless of design, they must receive sunlight for most of the day and have protection against wind. Keep them clear of trees and other garden plants that will compete for water and nutrients. If soil is heavy clay, beds should be raised and well drained to allow root growth and avoid waterlogging after heavy rains.

Soil preparation

Heavy soils, such as clay and clay loams, should not be worked while wet, but left to dry out to become crumbly. To improve these types of soil, add lime in the form of calcium carbonate or gypsum (calcium sulphate) which will improve the soil and allow other essential elements to be taken up by the plant. Organic matter in the form of manures, decaying straw, sawdust or garden compost is essential to condition heavy soils and encourage root penetration. It also provides some of the nutrients required by vegetables.

Sandy soils require very little digging but dry out quickly. This can be rectified by digging in and mulching with compost, spent mushroom compost or well-rotted manure. While some gardeners do not like the appearance, grass clippings make an excellent mulch and can be applied (but not too thickly) directly to the beds or added to the compost heap.

Maintaining pH levels

Most vegetables grow best in soils that have a pH range of between 6 and 7. The pH scale is one by which a soil's acidity or alkalinity is measured. It theoretically ranges between 1 and 14, pH7 representing neutral. Figures below pH7 indicate increasing acidity, those above, to pH14, increasing alkalinity.

In practice, most soils are rarely more acid than pH4.5, or more alkaline than pH8.5. The majority of vegetables, apart from brassicas and one or two others which enjoy limy soil, prefer neutral to slightly acid conditions. Use a pH testing kit, stocked by garden centres, to check your soil's acid/alkaline level.

Lime contains calcium, an essential plant food which also keeps soil sweet. It is quickly leached from soil in high rainfall areas, so sprinkle it over a different third of your plot each year. An application of between 50–100 grams per square metre (2–4oz per square yard) is usually sufficient. If you are a keen organic gardener, it is not advisable to mix lime with fresh manure. This causes a release of ammonia gas and consequent loss of nitrogen. Lime may also be returned to the soil by adding it, or wood ash, to the compost heap rather than digging it directly into the soil.

Some brands of lime-based fertiliser also contain quantities of trace elements. The uptake of trace elements and other nutrients only occurs within certain pH ranges. Nitrogen, phosphorus, calcium and magnesium for example, need a neutral to slightly alkaline pH range to be taken up. Iron, manganese and boron, however, need a slightly acidic soil. Nevertheless, even though pH levels may remain constant, it is humus and other decaying organic matter in the soil that bacteria feed upon which, in turn, makes nutrients and trace elements available to the plant. Diseases indicating these nutritional shortages will soon manifest themselves if the soil is not rich in humus.

Mulching

Mulch is the covering you place on garden soil to keep it healthy, to discourage weed growth and keep the surface and lower levels evenly cool. With heavy soils, it makes them less compact and therefore increases aeration. With sandy soils, it not only contributes nutrients but increases moisture absorption. Perforated black plastic sheeting is used to warm soils. An irrigation system under the sheet may have to be installed.

Organic mulching materials, such as leaves, garden compost, straw, lawn clippings and sawdust should be well rotted to ensure that bacteria do not have to work upon them. If they do, they will use up nitrogen which surrounding plants need. Top up organic mulches periodically, and occasionally apply a nitrogenous fertiliser to compensate for that which bacteria have drawn upon.

Fertilisers

Vegetables regularly require fertilisers. Composting is not the complete answer as it only contains those elements present in the composted material. Organic gardeners use only 'natural' products, such as blood, fish and bone and poultry and other animal manures, but these are usually low in phosphorus, with the exception of bonemeal. Compensate by applying chemical fertilisers such as superphosphate. Balanced branded fertilisers contain the three main elements required by plants for healthy growth: nitrogen (N), phosphorus (P) and potassium (K). They are applied at different times of the year and in varying quantities, depending on the type of vegetable grown, the composition of the soil and previous use of other fertilisers. The proportions in which these elements are combined is known as the NPK ratio. Complete fertilisers are usually applied before or at time of planting and should be thoroughly incorporated into the top 10cm (4in) of soil. Use about 50g (2oz) of fertiliser per metre of row.

Dressings of additional fertiliser scattered around the crop or the application of supplementary liquid fertilisers, which also contain trace elements needed by the plant, are usually required during the growing season.

CAPITALISE on space by intercropping fast-maturing crops such as lettuce between Brussels sprouts and other slower-growing vegetables.

A CAREFULLY PLANNED GARDEN will make the most effective use of the available space.

Raised beds

Raised-bed gardening is a compromise between beds and containers. It also solves the problem of localised poor soils and bad drainage. New soil should be about 30–45cm (12–18in) above the surrounding soil level and confined to beds approximately 1m (3ft) wide framed by railway sleepers, walling bricks, gravel boards or other strong construction material. Moisture levels in raised-bed gardens should be carefully monitored as the soil tends to dry out faster than in normal ground-level beds.

PLANNING YOUR CROPS

Higher yields will be obtained and a larger range of vegetables harvested if you put a little thought into planning what to grow. The following factors need to be considered.
● What is the microclimate like in your particular area?
● When is the best time for you to plant, and when should you harvest?
● Is it best for you to sow seeds or plant seedlings?
● How much space do you have, and is your soil suitable?

District

Choose crops according to the local climate in your area. Leafy crops, such as lettuce or cabbage, for example, may go to seed (bolt) in dry soil in a hot summer. On the other hand, if temperatures drop suddenly, some vegetables such as French beans may shed their flowers and fruits will not develop.

Planting and harvesting

Sowing and planting dates depend upon how hardy the plant is and how much it will tolerate cold weather. It is wise, therefore, to plan which crops are suitable for your particular area.

Harvesting dates, that is the number of days from sowing or planting to maturity, vary from vegetable to vegetable. Some can be picked early, some mid-season and others late in the season (see chart, pages 82–3).

VEGETABLES TO GROW OUTSIDE

Artichokes, globe and Jerusalem	Kale
	Kohl rabi
	Leek
Asparagus	Lettuce
Beans, broad,	Marrow
	Onion
French and runner	Parsnip
	Pea
Beetroot	Potato
Broccoli	Radish
Brussels sprouts	Rhubarb
	Salsify
Cabbage	Scorzonera
Carrots	Seakale
Cauliflower	Shallot
Celeriac/celery	Spinach
Chinese cabbage	Squash
	Swiss Chard
Courgette	Swede
Cucumber	Sweet corn
Endive	Tomato

Seeds and seedlings

The choice is yours and much depends on how much space and time you have. Seeds may be sown direct into cropping positions or raised to the seedling stage in seed beds, containers or seed boxes. Seedlings may be planted directly into the plot or into containers.

A general guide, if planting small seeds directly into the soil, is to open up a narrow planting row 10cm (4in) deep and 10cm (4in) wide. Spread complete fertiliser along the trench, then fill in with soil. Sow seeds on the soil, then cover with 1.3–1.9cm (0.5–0.75in) fertile soil containing coarse sand to prevent compaction and allow easy passage for germinating shoots. Alternatively, take out seed drills 1.3–1.9cm (0.5–0.75in) deep in soil in which you have raked in fertiliser 10 days previously. After sowing, tamp down the soil with the back of a rake and keep it moist but not wet. It may be necessary to water gently every day. After sowing in early spring, cover rows with fibre fleece to shield germinating seedlings from cold winds, heavy rain and pests.

Alternatively, seedlings can be raised in one of the many forms of container. The advantage is that you provide a protective and controlled environment for the developing plant. It will then be quite sturdy when you transplant it into the open garden. Cell trays are a popular choice as you can sow the seeds in individual compartments and then transplant the seedlings from the trays with no root check. If raising seedlings in seed trays or cell trays, use a multipurpose compost. When seedlings appear, boost growth by feeding weekly with a soluble form of complete fertiliser.

Siting – space, soil and support

An open sunny spot shielded from cold winds and well away from trees is vital. Watch which areas of the garden the sun reaches before choosing your vegetable plot. Make sure the plot is not shaded too much by fences, buildings or shrubbery. On sloping ground, beds may need supporting with sleepers or brick retaining walls. Check the condition of your soil: does it need fertilisers, manures or compost?

Use surrounding fences to support climbing beans or trailing cucumbers or squashes. Position taller plants, such as staked tomatoes, rhubarb, broad beans or Brussels sprouts where they won't shade smaller vegetables, such as carrots, beetroot and lettuce. Flower beds can be fringed with herbs such as parsley.

Consult seasonal growing charts to replace one quick-growing vegetable with another to ensure a constant supply of fresh produce from your vegetable garden.

Successional planting

Plan carefully where garden space is limited and you want to harvest a variety of crops from the same small area. Ideally, sow short rows of lettuce and radish fortnightly to ensure a regular supply and avoid a glut. Another way to maximise output is to intercrop: sowing fast developers, such as radish, early peas, early carrots, spinach and dwarf lettuce between rows of widely spaced and slow developing parsnips, Brussels sprouts and leeks. Use trellis space wisely, training against it peas, cucumbers, runner and climbing French beans.

In larger gardens, crop rotation, is advisable. Do not plant two successive crops of the same or related vegetable in the same area. For example, alternate root crops, such as carrots or beetroot, with leguminous vegetables such as peas or beans. Rotation of crops reduces the build-up of soil pests and diseases and encourages healthy growth.

Companion planting

Plant compatibility is the basis of companion planting. For years, gardeners have observed that some vegetables and herbs grow better when near each other while others, when combined, look sick or do not grow at all. In their natural environment many plants, left alone to self-seed from season to season, establish particular relationships, one with another. For example, small shallow-rooting plants grow in the shade of larger neighbours that protect them from hot sunshine.

The opposite to this can be seen in monocultures, such as market gardens or orchards, where the same types of plant are grown together to produce a specific crop. If a disease or pest,

VEGETABLES TO GROW UNDER GLASS

Aubergine	Lettuce
Capsicum/chilli	Okra
	Tomato
Chinese cabbage	
Cucumber	

WELL-PLANNED ROWS OF VEGETABLES make valuable use of limited garden areas and look very attractive. Alternatively, you may wish to have a more natural-looking vegetable garden where crops are planted in a less formal pattern.

particular to a variety, takes hold then an entire planting can be lost.

Many gardeners believe companion planting plays an important role in the control of pests and diseases in the vegetable garden. Some gardeners also maintain that it is better not to use artificial or chemically manufactured insecticides, herbicides and fungicides, and practice companion planting as an alternative.

Sometimes, to save a crop, the use of chemical sprays may be unavoidable. Wherever possible, use 'natural' sprays to keep your vegetables disease- and pest-free. Vegetables or herbs may exude 'natural' chemicals that either attract or repel insects or other plants. French marigolds are sometimes planted around tomatoes as they are believed to repel whitefly. Chives and garlic will repel aphids when planted near roses or deter the growth of apple scab when planted under apple trees.

CONTAINER GARDENS

Even in the smallest of spaces you can, given the right conditions, grow vegetables. Containers, which come in many shapes and sizes, are ideal.

The method is particularly important for those with physical disabilities, who are unable to work large gardens yet appreciate a supply of fresh produce near the house.

Planter boxes, wooden barrels, hanging baskets and terracotta, concrete or plastic pots are just some of the containers you can use. Here are some basic rules:
● Do not use galvanised containers or any pot with a narrow opening.
● Cheap plastic pots may deteriorate in strong sunlight and

terracotta pots dry out rapidly. Glazed ceramic pots are excellent but must have a good sized drainage hole.
● Wooden barrels or other timber containers should be treated with preservative before planting, to prevent rot.
● Use containers of between 15 litres (3.25 gals) and 120 litres (26 gals) litres capacity. Small pots restrict the root area and dry out very quickly. Deep-rooting vegetables require deep containers.
● Provide adequate drainage holes, about 1cm (0.5in) in diameter, and line the base of the pot with spent tea bags, crocks or pebbles to prevent loss of soil.
● Containers should be set on bricks or blocks to allow surplus water to drain away.
● Hanging baskets can be lined with layers of wool moss for water retention. Shelter the baskets from high winds. Some crops will benefit if the baskets are kept out of the afternoon sun, although some, such as 'Tumbler' tomatoes, will thrive in the sun.

Potting composts

Use a good quality multipurpose compost. Some also include a water-retaining gel. Most garden soils are usually unsuitable for container growing. The desired pH range is 5.6 to 7.0.

Cultivation

Fill the container with compost to within 5cm (2in) of the rim and plant seedlings – results are quicker than from seed. Set them 5cm (2in) from the edge of the container and firm compost around their roots.

Water regularly to speed growth. Unless you have added a slow-release feed to the compost, fertilisers need to be added

COURGETTES WILL GROW WELL in a medium-sized container, showing off their striking flowers and soft, attractive leaves.

throughout the growing period. Apply a high potash liquid fertiliser weekly. After planting, cover compost with a 2.5cm (1in) layer of well-rotted organic mulch, but keep it just clear of leafy vegetables, such as lettuce, spinach, Swiss chard and Chinese cabbage, which are susceptible to rot.

What to grow in containers

Small salad crops such as lettuce and mustard and cress, or larger vegetables including Swiss chard, which have a quick maturing period, are ideal. Cherry tomatoes and other fruiting kinds, including capsicum, can be easily grown in containers, as can root vegetables such as baby carrots, radishes and spring onions.

If you are growing tomatoes in growing bags, support cordon varieties with proprietary props that enclose the bag. Do not insert canes which will puncture the plastic. Ideally, site outdoor tomatoes against a warm, brick wall so warmth absorbed throughout the day is released at night to promote robust growth. But beware, tomatoes are prone to blight disease in humid and warm weather from mid July to August, so protect them by spraying with Bordeaux Mixture or some other copper-based fungicide, at the recommended intervals.

Aubergines also do well in growing bags as long as they have a sunny site.

Similar watering and feeding requirements apply to container-grown herbs. Grow faster-growing herbs around slower-growing vegetables such as broccoli.

COOKING VEGETABLES

Vegetables offer a nutritious and tasty way to balance one's diet and provide many vitamins and minerals essential to health. Nature ensures variety because a different vegetable

will reach its peak cropping time most months of the year. Let each season in turn provide you with cheap, flavoursome food.

Cooking times vary according to the method used and the quality, size, quantity and freshness of the vegetables. Whenever possible cook vegetables in their skins.
● The healthiest way to cook vegetables is in a microwave, using very little water. This will retain most nutrients. Washed leafy vegetables need no extra water when microwaved as the water in the leaves is sufficient.
● To steam, cook vegetables in an enclosed container suspended over a small amount of boiling water.
● Boiling involves completely immersing vegetables in boiling water or at least just covering them, and keeping the temperature constant until they are cooked. Water-soluble nutrients within the vegetables are leached out during this process, so do not waste the cooking water – use it later to make soups, stews and sauces.
● To parboil, boil vegetables for 5–8 minutes and then drain.
● Blanching involves covering the vegetable with boiling, salted water and cooking for a limited time. Vegetables are usually blanched before freezing (see individual entries in Freezing Vegetables, pages 78–81). Some, such as French beans, carrots, courgettes and peas, can be stored for a short time without blanching.
● Glazing involves cooking in a small quantity of water, sugar and butter until the mixture is reduced to a syrup; stir frequently to avoid scorching. Beetroot, radishes, onions, parsnips and carrots lend themselves to glazing.
● Pureeing vegetables is done in the food processor or blender, or by pressing through a sieve by hand. Pureed vegetables can be eaten at once, or stored in the freezer and reconstituted later.
● Other techniques include sautéeing and deep-frying. Both of these methods bring the vegetable into direct contact with hot oils, so are very quick methods of cooking. Roasting is a much slower process but gives a delicious flavour.

CHERRY TOMATOES AND BASIL grow companionably in plastic and ceramic container pots.

ASPARAGUS

Asparagus officinalis

FROM LATE APRIL to early June, use a serrated knife to cut emerging shoots when 12.5–17.5cm (5–7in) high, 7.5cm (3in) below the surface. Leave replacement shoots to form ferny-leaved stems to boost growth for next year.

FEATURES

Attractive, fern-like, feathery foliage is a feature of this hardy perennial which grows to 90–120cm (3–4ft) tall. The edible part of the plant is the tender young stem or spear. Male and female flowers grow on separate plants, with male plants producing larger and better spears. This delicious vegetable is easy to grow. Carefully cultivated, plants will crop heavily for at least 15 years.

CONDITIONS

Aspect Prefers full sun but will tolerate partial shade.
Site Needs well-drained neutral to limy soil. Lime acid plots. Not suitable for containers.

ASPARAGUS AT A GLANCE

A hardy perennial prized for its succulent new shoots (spears), which are harvested in spring.

		RECOMMENDED VARIETIES
JAN	/	
FEB	/	**Crowns:**
MAR	/	F1 'Boonlim'
APR	plant 🌱 harvest 🌿	'Connover's Colossal'
MAY	harvest 🌿	'Dariana'
JUN	harvest 🌿	'Franklim'
JULY	/	F1 'Geynlim'
AUG	/	'Lucullus'
SEPT	/	F1 'Venlim'
OCT	/	
NOV	/	
DEC	/	

GROWING METHOD

Sowing and planting Prepare permanent beds to a depth of 30cm (12in), adding plenty of organic matter and a complete fertiliser. Dig a trench 30cm (12in) wide and 20cm (8in) deep. Set one-year-old crowns 40cm (16in) apart in the trench and cover buds with 5cm (2in) of soil. As fern (foliage) grows, cover the crown with soil until the trench is filled, leaving new shoots uncovered. Fern dies off in winter and new shoots develop in spring. After planting, water copiously in dry spells. When fern yellows in autumn, cut it back to 5cm (2in) from the base. Don't gather spears the first year after planting to encourage the plants to establish. A mature clump will crop for 15 years or more.

Feeding Keep soil moist, especially when spears are forming. Dry soil causes stringy, woody stalks. Work in blood, fish and bone meal in spring and early summer to encourage robust growth.

Problems Asparagus beetle, about 6mm (0.25in) long and recognised by orange markings, chews leaves and stems. Spray with insecticide when first seen.

HARVESTING

Picking Gather spears the second spring after planting. Harvesting may last up to 8 weeks, between April and June. Cut when spears are 15–20cm (6–8in) long, at or just below soil level, being careful not to damage adjacent new shoots. Feathering of spear means harvest is too late. Harvest along the same row at two week intervals. For white asparagus, cut spears 15cm (6in) below soil level when the tip has just reached the soil surface. Production increases annually and maturity occurs at 4–5 years.

AUBERGINE
Solanum melongena

GROWN IN rich soil, growing bags or pots, aubergines crop freely. Water and feed regularly and pick when 12.5–15cm (5–6in) long.

FEATURES

Aubergines, also called eggplants, can make bushes to 1.5m (5ft) tall with large, coarse, hairy, grey-green leaves. The star-shaped flowers are mauve with yellow centres. A bush produces 5–6 fruits which take 3–4 months to develop. The fruit of different varieties varies in shape and size from long and slender to egg-shaped. The colour may be dark purple to black or creamy white. Some are even striped.

CONDITIONS

Aspect   Aubergines are more successful in a greenhouse than outdoors, but may succeed under cloches in warm, sunny gardens.

Site   If growing aubergines outdoors, under cloches, the soil must be well drained and rich in organic matter. Dig in bulky organic materials in autumn or winter. Aubergines grow very well in large pots or growing bags.

GROWING METHOD

Sowing and planting   Raise seedlings in February or March. Set two seeds per small peat pot, water in and germinate in a temperature of 16–21°C. Thin each pair to the strongest seedling and grow plants in good light. When the seedlings are 12.5–15cm (5–6in) high, transplant them one to a 22.5cm (9in) pot or three to a standard sized growing bag. Alternatively, harden off and plant out 60cm (2ft) apart each way in late May or early June, when frosts have finished. Nip out the growing tip to encourage branching when the stem is 30cm (12in) high. Mist plants to deter red spider mites. Cut off side shoots and remaining flowers when five fruits have formed.

Feeding   Feed greenhouse plants weekly with a liquid feed of a high potash fertiliser when flowers have been pollinated and fruits start to swell. A few days before planting outdoor plants, prepare soil by raking in 56g per sq m (2oz per sq yd) of balanced fertiliser such as blood, fish and bone meal or Growmore. This will speed robust leafy growth. To encourage a good crop, practise the greenhouse technique of liquid feeding with a potash rich fertiliser when fruits set. Do not overwater as plants are susceptible to root rot. Maintain even moisture and temperature levels in the soil by mulching, Watering may be increased as plants mature.

Problems   Aphids, whitefly and spider mites are the main pests. Treat with appropriate sprays. Crop rotation may be necessary to lessen the incidence of soil-borne wilt diseases. However, do not grow capsicum or tomatoes in succession with aubergines. Leaf spot and fruit rot can be controlled by fungicidal sprays.

HARVESTING

Picking   Pick the fruit when 12.5–15cm (5–6in) long and well coloured, and before the seeds harden and turn brown. The skin should be tight, firm and unwrinkled. Over-ripe fruit is coarse and bitter. Cut the stems with secateurs to remove the fruit without damaging them.

AUBERGINE AT A GLANCE

Also known as eggplant, and grown in a greenhouse or outdoors, the large purple or white fruits form on prickly stems.

		RECOMMENDED VARIETIES
JAN	/	
FEB	/	'Bandera'
MAR	sow	'Black Bell'
APR	transplant	'Black Emperor'
MAY	sow, transplant	F1 'Bonica'
JUN	/	'Long Purple'
JULY	harvest	'Mini Bambino'
AUG	harvest	'Moneymaker'
SEPT	harvest	'Slice Rite'
OCT	harvest	
NOV	/	
DEC	/	

BEAN, RUNNER
Phaseolus vulgaris

HELP RUNNER BEANS flower well and set an abundance of pods by liquid feeding with a high-potash fertiliser and keeping soil moist.

UNLIKE RUNNER BEANS, whose pods are long and thin, French varieties are shorter and rounded.

FEATURES

Climbing and dwarf bean varieties have leaves that are composed of three small leaflets which are quite nutritious when picked and used in salads. Edible flowers come in a variety of colours. The immature pod is the principal edible part of this versatile half-hardy perennial vegetable which is grown as an annual. There are stringed and stringless forms. Climbing beans give a heavier crop over a longer period than dwarf varieties.

CONDITIONS

Aspect
Site
Prefers sunny spots where the soil is warm. Soil should be well drained and fertilised. Dig in plenty of organic matter in poor plots. Lime acid soil. Mulch with compost to protect the shallow root system and promote water retention. When weeding, take care not to disturb the soil or roots just beneath the surface. Most varieties are suitable for growing in medium to large containers.

GROWING METHOD

Sowing and planting
Raise seedlings in gentle heat in April, harden them off and transplant them into prepared soil in May when frosts finish. Enjoy a succession of pods by sowing further crops outdoors in May and June. If raising plants under glass, set one seed per 7.5cm (3in) pot of multipurpose compost. When sowing outdoors, set seeds 5cm (2in) deep and 15cm (6in) apart

in double rows 45cm (18in) apart. Grow plants over a framework of netting or criss-crossed canes to a height of 1.8–2.4m (6–8ft). If space is restricted, make a pyramid of 6–8 canes for plants to canopy. Encourage pods to set by keeping the soil moist and mulching thickly with rotted manure or compost. The growing season is short, around 10–12 weeks, and with high temperatures (over 27°C) pods may not set. Dwarf beans mature more quickly than climbing varieties, so stagger your planting.

Feeding
If the soil is very acid work in 113g per square metre (4oz per square yard) of lime about a month before sowing. Apply a balanced fertiliser either side of young plants. Or, rake in 57g per square metre (2oz per square yard)

RUNNER BEAN AT A GLANCE

Half hardy perennial climbers yielding heavy crops of tender pods from summer to early autumn.

		RECOMMENDED VARIETIES
JAN	/	**Stringless:**
FEB	/	'Armstrong'
MAR	/	'Desiree'
APR	sow	'Fergie'
MAY	sow, transplant	'Kelvedon Stringless'
JUN	sow	
JULY	harvest	**Standard:**
AUG	harvest	'Enorma'
SEPT	harvest	'Prizewinner'
OCT	/	'Scarlet Emperor'
NOV	/	'White Emergo'
DEC	/	

*TIGHT FOR SPACE? Grow runner beans up a wigwam of canes —
on the vegetable plot or in a flower border.*

*THOUGH THERE ARE bush varieties of runner bean, their pods are
not as straight as dwarf French beans.*

of fertiliser ten days before sowing. Apply
liquid fertiliser when flowering commences.
In sandy soils, watering is essential as beans
have shallow root systems. Seeds sown in moist
soils do not require further watering until the
seedlings appear. At flowering time, beans like
humid conditions. Ideally, water at dusk or at
night, with a seep hose placed between a
double row of plants, or inside a pyramid, so
little moisture is lost by evaporation.

Problems Aphids and red spider mite (in spring to late
summer) and bean fly are the main pests, with
blight mosaic and anthracnose being diseases to
watch for. Control pests by spraying or dusting
with insecticides, especially on undersides of
leaves. Don't leave dead plant material lying
around, to avoid spreading disease. Seasonally
rotate crops to prevent the spread of fungi.

HARVESTING

Picking Pods are ready for picking in 12–14 weeks
from sowing. Frequent picking will result in
increased flowering and greater yields. Be
careful not to be too energetic when pulling off
the pods, to avoid damaging the stems. The
pods are ready to pick when they snap easily
between the fingers and seeds are not yet fully
developed. Pick off any pods which are too old
and too large for eating, as retaining them will
inhibit the production of new pods.

*'STREAMLINE' was first introduced in 1935, and has been one of
the most popular varieties of runner bean for more than 50 years.*

BEETROOT

Beta vulgaris

TENDER YOUNG red-veined beetroot leaves are tasty and nutritious when cooked like spinach and served as greens.

DIG MAINCROP ROOTS in autumn for storing over winter. Twist off leaves 5cm (2in) from the crown and pack roots in a box of sand.

FEATURES

Beetroot is mostly cultivated as an annual vegetable. The swollen edible root can be globular or tapered and is red, yellow (Golden Beet) or white. The leaves sprout as a rosette above ground and, when young, are delicious in salads. Beetroot is suitable for growing in fertilised garden beds or large containers; however, the long, cylindrical maincrop varieties are not suitable for growing in containers.

CONDITIONS

Aspect Can tolerate both sun and partial shade.
Site Prefers loose soils, which allow roots to grow freely. Soils need to be high in organic matter, well limed and with good drainage.

BEETROOT AT A GLANCE

A perennial, grown as an annual, beetroot has plump roots that are lifted from summer to autumn.

		RECOMMENDED VARIETIES
JAN	/	
FEB	sow	Globe rooted:
MAR	sow	'Boltardy'
APR	sow	'Burpee's Golden'
MAY	sow	'Detroit 2 – Little Ball'
JUN	harvest	'Detroit 2 – New
JULY	sow harvest	Globe'
AUG	harvest	
SEPT	harvest	Long rooted:
OCT	harvest	'Forono'
NOV	/	
DEC	/	

GROWING METHOD

Sowing For early crops, set seeds in cloche-warmed soil from late February to March. Continue with unprotected sowings from mid April to May and finish with a late May or early June sowing for lifting maincrop roots, for winter storage, in October. Enjoy tender young roots in autumn by sowing 'Detroit-Early-Ball' in July. Dig and crumble soil and firm gently by shuffling over it. Rake it level and take out seed drills 2.5cm (1in) deep and 30cm (12in) apart. Sow thinly or space pairs of seed 10cm (4in) apart. Alternatively, take out trenches 10cm (4 in) deep, 8cm (3in) wide and 30cm (12in) apart. Sprinkle a narrow band of complete fertiliser in the trench and cover with 5cm (2in) of soil. Sow seeds on top and cover with 2.5cm (1in) of soil. Alternatively, rake a complete fertiliser into the bed before sowing. Thin very young seedlings to 2.5cm (1in) apart and later to 9cm (3.5in) as the roots swell. Beet do not like weed competition but, when weeding, take care not to damage developing roots.

Feeding Do not over manure or fertilise soils in beds that have been heavily fertilised for the previous crop, as this leads to rather tasteless beetroot with a low sugar content. Give young beet plenty of water to encourage larger, tender roots. Left to dry out, the vegetable becomes tough and stringy.

Problems Seldom any problems.

HARVESTING

Lifting Beets mature approximately 3–4 months after sowing, depending on the area and seasonal conditions. Pull alternate roots when golf ball size and leave remainder to mature.

BROAD BEAN

Vicia faba

PINCH OUT SHOOT TIPS when the first tier of pods begins to swell, to deter blackfly from colonising plants.

FEATURES

A hardy annual growing to 1.2m (4ft) tall, it has square stems producing small leaflets which give the plant a bushy look. White flowers in spring and summer later produce 15–20cm (6–8in) pods containing edible seeds. The seeds are large and are normally used fresh. When plants are developing and forming pods, shoot tips may also be eaten. Beheading plants in this manner encourages pods to fill out more quickly. Broad beans are ideal for small gardens but not suited to container growing.

CONDITIONS

Aspect
Site

Likes full sunlight and shelter from cold winds. Best in soil that is well drained and rich in organic matter. Broad beans grow best in neutral to alkaline soil. If a pH test indicates acidity, raise the pH by raking garden lime into the bed in autumn or winter.

GROWING CONDITIONS

Sowing and planting

Set seeds in late October or November in a sheltered well-drained plot, for harvesting pods in June. Sow again in March, and monthly until June for a succession of pods. Take out double drills 5cm (2in) deep and 20cm (8in) apart and set seeds alternately 20cm (8in) apart. Leave 60cm (2ft) between each pair of rows. Hoe regularly to check weeds, and nip out shoot tips of spring or early summer sown plants to deter blackfly. Broad beans require only limited attention during the 4–5 months growing season which plants take to reach maturity. If lower pods are swelling nicely, shoot tips can be nipped out to hasten maturity.

Feeding

As with other pulses, broad beans add atmospheric nitrogen to the soil through the action of nitrogen-fixing bacteria in root nodules. When preparing beds rake in a balanced fertiliser at the rate of 112g per square metre (4oz per square yard). Do not overwater broad beans as wet soil combined with high temperatures leads to root diseases. Normally, seeds planted in damp soil require no further watering until seedlings appear about two weeks later. As plants mature, water only when soil starts to dry out. Water copiously if soil is dry when pods are swelling.

Problems

Blackfly, a tiny soft-bodied sucking insect, is the main pest and should be controlled by spraying with pirimicarb when first seen. Diseases include chocolate spot, which causes brownish black blotches to appear on leaves. Control by spraying with fungicide and avoid using high nitrogen fertiliser. Crop rotation over several seasons will lessen the incidence of disease.

HARVESTING

Picking

Young pods are harvested from early summer. Whole pods containing half-ripe seeds can be prepared and eaten as you would climbing beans. Otherwise, gather pods when seeds are quite large but not bulging.

BROAD BEAN AT A GLANCE

A hardy annual grown for its crop of plump seeds contained in fat pods. Young pods and shoot tips are delicious too.

Month	Activity	RECOMMENDED VARIETIES
JAN	/	**Spring sown:**
FEB	/	'Dreadnought'
MAR	sow	'Express'
APR	sow	'Hylon'
MAY	sow	'Imperial White Windsor'
JUN	sow harvest	'Stereo'
JULY	harvest	'The Sutton'
AUG	harvest	
SEPT	harvest	**Autumn sown:**
OCT	/	'Aquadulce'
NOV	sow	
DEC	/	

BROCCOLI

Brassica oleracea var. *italica*

CALABRESE: cut the large cntral head (cluster of flower buds) before petals appear. This will trigger a profusion of secondary heads.

FEATURES

Grown as annuals, there are purple sprouting, white sprouting and green sprouting (calabrese or Italian) forms of broccoli. Green sprouting varieties initially resemble a cauliflower until the central head is cut and side shoots appear.

CONDITIONS

Aspect
Purple and white sprouting varieties are hardiest and prosper in full sun and cold areas. Calabrese crops from autumn to first frosts and needs a warmer position.

Site
Likes a neutral to alkaline soil with a pH of 6.5–7.5. Add manures and fertilisers, providing extra nitrogen if soil is sandy and impoverished. Calabrese can also be grown in containers.

GROWING METHOD

Sowing and planting
Purple and white sprouting: Sow thinly on a limed seed bed from April to May, transplanting seedlings when 15cm (6in) high in June and July. Set plants 45cm (18in) apart each way in fertilised soil.
Calabrese: This is best sown direct in the cropping site from late March or April to early July. Sow in drills 60cm (2ft) apart and thin seedlings to 15cm (6in) apart. Close spacing results in small but acceptable curds (heads). Initial rapid leaf growth will occur, followed by development of the edible head in about 3–4 months. Side shoots develop after the central head has been harvested. New growth is encouraged if the base of the plant and some outer leaves are left on after cropping.

Feeding
Feed plants during the growing season by applying side dressings of fish, blood and bone meal. Weekly applications of liquid seaweed fertiliser also improve crops. Broccoli grows quickly so keep soil moist by constant watering. Cut down on watering as heads mature. Lack of moisture leads to seeding without head formation. Enrich soil by digging in old manure or garden compost in autumn.

Problems
Broccoli is quite prone to disease. The risk will be reduced by seasonal crop rotation. The main insect pests are larvae of cabbage moth and cabbage white butterfly. These can be controlled by spraying with *Bacillus thuringiensis* (a bioinsecticide). Curling of the leaf, a disease known as whip tail, is an indication of a trace element (molybdenum) shortage. Correct this deficiency by watering seedlings either before or after transplanting with a solution containing 5g (0.2oz) sodium molybdate in 5 litres (10 pints) water. Downy mildew is also a condition to watch for in moist cool areas. If this is a problem see that there is a good air flow and that the plants receive maximum sunlight. Net plants against pigeons in winter.

HARVESTING

Picking
Purple and white sprouting broccoli: Gather embryo flower shoots (spears) when well developed but unopened, from February to April. Pick them when they are young and tender to encourage rapid succession.
Calabrese: Cut the central head from August to October to encourage a lots of side shoots.

BROCCOLI AT A GLANCE

Calabrese forms a cauliflower-like head for cutting in summer. Sprouting broccoli is grown for its spears, harvested in spring.

Month	Activity		RECOMMENDED VARIETIES
JAN	/		
FEB	/		**Calabrese:**
MAR	/		'Corvet'
APR	sow	🌱	Early Romanesco'
MAY	sow	🌱	'El Centro'
JUN	sow	🌱	'Green Sprouting'
JULY	/		F1 'Mercedes'
AUG	harvest	🌿	'Royal Banquet'
SEPT	harvest	🌿	'F1 'Shogun'
OCT	harvest	🌿	'Trixie'
NOV	/		**Purple sprouting:**
DEC	/		'Purple sprouting early'
			'Purple sprouting late'

BRUSSELS SPROUT

Brassica oleracea var. *gemmifera*

F1 HYBRIDS, as pictured, are the heaviest croppers, but older, standard kinds can be harvested over a longer period.

FEATURES

The Brussels sprout is a member of the cabbage family, with similar requirements to those of cabbages. The small heads (buttons) measure approximately 2.5cm (1in) in diameter and sprout from a tall main stem among large green leaves. The growing season is long, from 28 weeks for early varieties to 36 weeks for late kinds. If you prefer all the sprouts on a stem to mature at the same time grow F1 hybrid varieties. Open-pollinated varieties such as 'Bedford' are harvested over a longer period.

CONDITIONS

Aspect
Beds should have a sunny aspect. Protect plants from wind damage by mounding soil around plants during the growing period.

Site
Brussels sprouts are very hardy but will not grow in waterlogged soils. Most soils are suitable with the exception of sandy soils which produce only loose leafy buttons with no heart.

GROWING METHOD

Sowing and planting
For extra early crops, raise seedlings in gentle heat in February, harden off and transplant when 10–12.5cm (4–5in) tall. Most varieties are sown outdoors in a nursery bed, in drills 1.3cm (0.5in) deep and 15cm (6in) apart, in fertile soil, limed if acid, from March to April. Cloche rows in chilly districts. Set plants out from May to June, 75cm (2.5ft) apart each way. Make sure seedlings have distinct growing points. If blind, reject them. As they grow, stake plants on windy plots, and remove yellowing leaves to improve air flow.

Feeding
Prepare final cropping quarters some weeks ahead of transplanting by digging in bulky organic manure in autumn or winter. Rake in a balanced fertiliser before sowing. Extra nitrogen should be added by feeding with sulphate of ammonia in late summer. If heavy rains have leached nutrients from the soil, apply sulphate of potash. Water frequently as plants need a great deal to encourage growth. Ease off in late summer.

Problems
Cabbage moth causes problems early in the season and later aphids, slugs and snails may damage sprouts. Control these pests with proprietory sprays and baits. Club root (accentuated by acidic soils) is best controlled by rotation of crops and dipping seedling roots in thiophanate methyl before transplanting. Yellowish areas around leaves indicate magnesium deficiency. Water soil around plant with a solution of 28g (1oz) magnesium sulphate (Epsom salts) in 4.55 litres (1 gallon) water.

HARVESTING

Picking
Harvest is from early autumn through to spring. Pick buttons, a few from each plant in turn, before they burst. Start at the bottom of the stem where mature sprouts first develop. When all buttons have been gathered, cut off cabbagy tops and steam them. They have a delicious flavour. When picking, also remove leaves that have turned yellow to encourage air flow round plants and reduce risk of fungal infection.

BRUSSELS SPROUT AT A GLANCE

A hardy brassica whose sprouts (buttons), sweeter after being frosted, form thickly on the stem from late summer to spring.

Month	Activity		RECOMMENDED VARIETIES
JAN	harvest		F1 'Oliver'
FEB	sow		F1 'Masterline'
MAR	sow		F1 'Peer Gynt'
APR	sow, transplant		'Bedford' (open
MAY	transplant		pollinated)
JUN	transplant		F1 'Proline'
JULY	/		F1 'Rampart'
AUG	/		F1 'Topline'
SEPT	harvest		'Uniline'
OCT	harvest		
NOV	harvest		
DEC	harvest		

CABBAGE
Brassica oleracea var. *capitata*

'RUBY BALL' is an autumn-maturing cabbage that hearts well and has few wasted leaves.

FEATURES

The edible head of the cabbage is a large terminal bud composed of many tightly packed, overlapping leaves forming a round or sometimes pointed head.

Spring cabbage: Sown from July to August, heads or spring greens are ready for cutting from February to June. Cloche plants over winter in cold gardens.

Summer cabbage: Raised under cloches, or outdoors from late winter to spring, heads are harvested from June to October.

Winter cabbage: These include round-headed varieties, crinkly-leaved Savoys and red-leaved kinds. Sown in April or May, they yield chunky heads from autumn to winter. Red cabbage is less hardy than other autumn and winter kinds and is cut from September to November.

CONDITIONS

Aspect   Finest heads are produced by plants that are in full sun and sheltered from cold winds.

Site   Prefers well-drained, alkaline soil made fertile with the addition of well-rotted manure.

GROWING METHOD

Sowing and planting   Spring, summer and winter varieties are raised in a well-prepared seedbed. Crumble soil and rake to a fine tilth, work in lime if the soil is acid, and add a balanced fertiliser. Take out seed drills 1.3cm (0.5in) deep and 15cm (6in) apart and sow seeds thinly. Firm soil over them and water if soil is dry. Thin seedlings to 2.5cm (1in) apart to encourage robust growth. When seedlings are 10–12.5cm (4–5in) high, with five or six leaves, move them to their cropping positions. Set spring cabbage 10cm (4in) apart in rows 30cm (12in) apart. In spring, thin to 20cm (8in) and use thinnings as spring greens. Set summer and winter cabbage 30–45cm (12–18in) apart, depending on variety.

Feeding   Cabbages like a lot of watering, so keep topsoil moist at all times. They prefer slightly alkaline soils. If the soil is acid, apply garden lime and a balanced fertiliser several weeks before planting. Spread small amounts of the same fertiliser around plants one month after planting and water in at once. When cabbages start to form firm hearts, apply a light dressing of Nitro Chalk, especially if the soil is sandy.

Problems   Various caterpillars attack cabbages, including those of the cabbage moth and cabbage white. Control with insecticide. Club root can be a problem (see page 19). Tackle cabbage root fly by dusting seed drills and around seedlings with primiphos methyl. Beat cabbage aphids by spraying with pirimicarb when first seen. Net plants against pigeons in winter.

HARVESTING

Cutting   Spring varieties take around 30 weeks to mature, but summer and winter kinds can be ready for cutting in 25 weeks from seed. Harvest red and winter white cabbages in November, remove outer leaves, store them in boxes of straw in a frost-free but airy shed.

CABBAGE AT A GLANCE

Grown as a hardy annual, the combination of spring, summer and winter varieties ensures a year-round supply.

		RECOMMENDED VARIETIES
JAN	harvest	**Spring:**
FEB	sow	'Durham Early'
MAR	sow	F1 'Spring Hero'
APR	harvest	
MAY	sow, transplant	**Summer:**
JUN	sow, transplant	F1 'Cape Horn'
JULY	sow	F1 'Derby Day'
AUG	harvest	
SEPT	transplant	
OCT	harvest	**Winter:**
NOV	harvest	F1 'Tundra'
DEC	harvest	'January King'

CABBAGE VARIETIES

Red cabbage:
Delicious pickled, cooked, or shredded into winter salads, and will stand in the garden well into the New Year.

Black or palm cabbage Black Tuscany':
A handsome, well-flavoured variety with very dark, narrow leaves, also listed under kale.

White ballhead cabbage:
Impressive quality and flavour. Will keep many weeks when cut if stored in a cool place.

Spring cabbage:
Young leafy heads can be enjoyed for many months of the year by sowing at regular intervals.

Winter ballhead:
Extremely hardy with a sweet, crisp texture. Can be cropped from October to February.

Savoy cabbage:
Beautiful, crinkled, dark green heads are very hardy.

CAPSICUM & CHILLIES

Capsicum annuum

PICK SWEET PEPPERS green. If left to ripen and turn red they will check the development of further fruits.

CHARACTERISTICALLY CONE-SHAPED chilli peppers – ideal for curries, pickles and sauces – keep for up to three weeks in a fridge.

FEATURES

Capsicum and chillies, known as sweet and hot peppers respectively, are perennials often grown as annuals. Capsicum may be roundish or long, flat and twisted, and green, red, yellow to white, or purple to dark chocolate in colour. Both crop best in a greenhouse but can be grown, under cloches, on a warm, sunny site. The chilli is noted for its hotness; the capsicum has a delicate, sweet, mild flavour.

CONDITIONS

Aspect   Need plenty of warmth and full sun.

CAPSICUM AND CHILLI AT A GLANCE

Perennials treated as annuals, they form blocky or cone-shaped fruits from mid summer to autumn.

JAN	/	RECOMMENDED VARIETIES	
FEB	/		
MAR	sow	**Capsicum:**	
APR	transplant	F1 'Big Bertha'	
MAY	transplant	F1 'Canape'	
JUN	/	'Jingle Bells'	
JULY	harvest		
AUG	harvest	**Chillies:**	
SEPT	harvest	'Anaheim'	
OCT	harvest	F1 'Hero'	
NOV	/	'Chilli Serrano'	
DEC	/	F1 'Super Cayenne'	

Site   Fertile soil, rich in organic matter.

GROWING METHOD

Sowing and planting   If growing plants outdoors, make sure the bed faces south and warms up quickly. Raise plants in March or April by sowing two or three seeds per 7.5cm (3in) pot of multipurpose compost, and germinating in a gently heated propagator. Thin seedlings to the strongest. If growing in a greenhouse, transfer stocky seedlings to growing bags, three to a bag, or one to a 22.5cm (9in) pot. If planting outside, wait until frosts finish in spring and set plants in cloche-warmed soil, 38–45 cm (15–18in) apart.
Mist flowers of greenhouse plants to encourage fruits to set and keep down red spider mite. Support stems with canes or tie to wires.

Feeding   Liquid feed greenhouse plants weekly when fruits set. Outdoors, apply a balanced fertiliser to beds a week before planting. After flowering and when fruit has set, apply a weekly feed of high potash liquid fertiliser. Keep plants evenly watered to prevent flower drop.

Problems   Aphids are the main pests. Control them by spraying with insecticide. Watch out for powdery mildew and apply a fungicide if white mould is seen. Crop rotation is advisable if soil-borne diseases, such as wilt, occur.

HARVESTING

Picking   Capsicum and chilli take 3–4 months to mature. Chillies may be picked at any colour stage but will be hotter if left to ripen fully.

CARROT

Daucus carota

CARROTS THRIVE in a sunny position on organically rich sandy loam. On shallow, stony soils grow stump- or globe-rooted varieties.

FEATURES

A perennial grown as an annual. Spherical and short varieties may be grown in containers but the long varieties growing to 20cm (8in) or more require friable soil in the open garden. 'Baby' carrots are immature roots pulled when grown no more than 10cm (4in) long and 1.25cm (0.5in) in diameter. The root of the carrot is a strong reddish orange, producing a feathery green rosette of leaves at soil level.

CONDITIONS

Aspect
Site

Likes full sun but tolerates partial shade. Prefers a cool, moist bed of friable soil where well-rotted organic matter was added for a previous crop. Roots grow well without blemishes in sandy or loamy soils. Add lime if soil is acid. This improves root colour. Keep bed free of weeds but avoid hoeing deeply to protect the developing roots. Mulch to keep soil temperatures cool.

GROWING METHOD

Sowing and planting

It's easy to raise a succession of crops. Sow a stump-rooted variety in cloche-warmed soil in early March, for lifting in June. For roots in July, set seeds in a sheltered spot from March to April. For maincrop roots, for harvesting from September to October and eating fresh, sow from mid April to early June. A succulent crop of 'new' carrots can be yours to enjoy if you sow a stump-rooted variety in August and cloche seedlings in October. When seedlings are about 5cm (2in) high, thin to 2.5cm (1in) apart. When remaining seedlings reach 15cm (6in), thin again to 5cm (2in) apart. Discarded plants are eaten as 'baby' carrots.

Feeding

Do not over-fertilise garden beds. Beds that have been heavily manured the previous season are ideal, which is something to keep in mind when rotating crops. If necessary, rake in a complete fertiliser a week before sowing, at a rate of 14g per square metre (0.5oz per square yard). Too much nitrogen leads to excessive leaf growth and poor coloured roots. Watering is important for growing good quality carrots. Small amounts only are required during the first eight weeks of seedling growth. This forces a desirable downwards growth of the roots. Water heavily only if soil dries out as the crop matures. Too much water induces roots to crack.

Problems

Control carrot root fly, without spraying, by covering sown rows with fibre fleece, or by sowing a resistant variety, such as 'Fly Away'. If you live in a bad carrot fly area, you can reduce the risk of attack to some extent by timing sowings to avoid egg hatching times.

HARVESTING

Lifting

The good thing about carrots is they can be cropped at whatever size you want them. Full maturity is reached approximately 12–16 weeks after sowing, depending on variety and area. To harvest, use a garden fork and lift roots gently from the ground when soil is moist to prevent the roots from snapping. Lift roots in October for storing, and cut off leaves 2.5cm (1in) from the crown. Pack them in boxes, interleaving them with moist sand. Keep in a cool, frost-free shed.

CARROT AT A GLANCE

A succession of sowings from March to August yields a year-round supply of roots for eating fresh or storing for later.

Month	Activity		RECOMMENDED VARIETIES
JAN	/		
FEB	/		'Amsterdam Sweetheart'
MAR	sow		'Chantenay Red Cored'
APR	sow		'Nantes Express'
MAY	sow		'Fly Away'
JUN	sow	harvest	'St Valery'
JULY	sow	harvest	'Ingot'
AUG	sow	harvest	'James' Scarlet Intermediate'
SEPT	harvest		'Autumn King'
OCT	harvest		F1 'Ingot'
NOV	harvest		
DEC	harvest		

CAULIFLOWER

Brassica oleracea var. *botrytis*

BEND A LEAF or two over developing curds to shield summer cauliflowers from hot sunshine and winter varieties from frost or snow.

FEATURES

Grown as an annual, this plant has a single stalk supporting a solid head made up of edible flower buds. Heads can be white, green or purple, depending upon variety. Both early and late maturing types are available. 'Mini' varieties are now on the market and require much less space than larger cauliflowers. Cauliflowers are not suited to container growing. The colour of white cauliflowers is preserved by protecting heads from sunlight or frost. The best way to shield heads from heat or cold is to break a leaf over them.

CONDITIONS

Aspect
Need to be protected from both full sunlight and frosts or maturing heads will discolour.

Site
Cauliflowers have large root systems and are not suited to container growing. As they are heavy feeders, beds need plenty of organic matter, and plants need feeding frequently.

GROWING METHOD

Sowing and planting
Summer varieties: Raise seedlings in gentle heat in January or February and grow on singly in pots. Alternatively, set seeds on a limed nursery bed, in drills 1.3cm (0.5in) deep and 15cm (6in) apart, in April. Move sturdy young plants to their cropping position in June. Gather heads in late summer or early autumn. Autumn varieties: Raise in a seed bed outdoors from April to mid May and plant out in late June. Harvest from September to November. Winter/spring varieties: Sow seeds in May, move young plants to cropping quarters in July and cut heads from February to May. Seedlings take about ten days to appear and are ready for transplanting when around 10–12cm (4–5in) high. Space at least 60cm (2ft) apart. Transplant only in cool weather.

Feeding
Keep soil moist around maturing plants to assist head development, but avoid watering directly over the head which can damage it. The head may also need protection from heavy rainfall. Before planting, enrich soil with a balanced fertiliser. If your soil is acid, raise its pH by applying lime. Lime also assists in the taking up of the trace element molybdenum. A balanced fertiliser can be applied 4 weeks after transplanting seedlings. Cauliflowers will take more manure and fertilisers than other members of the *Brassica* family. Dressings of nitrogenous fertiliser will promote growth if applied when heads are starting to form.

Problems
Caterpillars of the cabbage white butterfly, and aphids, are a problem. Treat with a proprietory pesticide. Cauliflowers also suffer from club root (see p.19) and cabbage root fly (see p.20). Net plants against pigeons in winter.

HARVESTING

Cutting
Harvesting usually takes place 18–24 weeks from sowing for summer and autumn varieties, and 40–50 weeks for winter kinds. Remove heads when about 20cm (8in) wide, by cutting before they become discoloured and lose their crisp firmness. Young leaves can also be harvested and used as greens for cooking.

CAULIFLOWER AT A GLANCE

Grown as a summer, autumn or winter maturing annual, its firm white flowerhead (curd) forms within a rosette of leaves.

			RECOMMENDED VARIETIES
JAN	sow		
FEB	sow		**Summer/autumn:**
MAR	sow, transplant		F1 'Beauty'
APR	harvest		F1 'Canberra'
MAY	sow		'Lateman'
JUN	sow	harvest	'White Ball'
JULY	transplant		
AUG	harvest		**Winter/spring:**
SEPT	harvest		'Early Feltham'
OCT	harvest		'Fleurly'
NOV	harvest		'Purple Cape'
DEC	/		'Walcheren Winter 3'

CELERIAC

Apium graveolens rapaceum

CELERY-FLAVOURED and vitamin-rich, celeriac tastes best if eaten freshly dug. Slice or shred it for salads or dice it and use it in cooking.

FEATURES

A curious and little-grown biennial rich in calcium, phosphorus and vitamin C, celeriac was introduced into Britain from Europe in the early eighteenth century. Also known as turnip-rooted celery – its leaf bases fuse into a solid globe which swells to the size of a grapefruit – celeriac is hardier, more disease resistant and easier to grow than its close cousin celery. Characteristically, it forms a topknot of celery-shaped leaves. To excel and form large succulent globes celeriac needs a long, unchecked growing season.

CONDITIONS

Aspect
In nature, it grows in permanently moist soil in bright sunlight or very light shade, so try and simulate these requirements. It should also be sheltered from cold winds.

Site
The soil must be deep, humus-rich and moisture retentive but not liable to waterlogging. Light sandy or sandy loam soils are suitable if you improve moisture retention by incorporating in autumn and winter a barrow load per square metre of crumbly manure or well-rotted garden compost. The organic materials that have been added will then break down over winter and release plant foods to speed robust growth the following season.

GROWING METHODS

Sowing and planting
This crop needs a long growing season, so start early – in February or March. Set seeds thinly and shallowly in pots of multipurpose compost and germinate them in a propagator heated to around 18°C. Germination tends to be sporadic, so prick out seedlings when they appear and the moment you can handle them. Set them singly into expanding Jiffy peat pots

or 5cm (2in) apart into seed trays. Keep them growing strongly in a temperature of 13–16°C.

If you haven't a heated greenhouse or bright, warm windowsill, delay sowing until April, when seedlings can be raised outdoors in an unheated frame or in cloches sealed at the ends. Being half-hardy, it's vital to toughen up seedlings before transplanting them when frosts finish in late May or early June. Give youngsters a good start by raking in 56g per square metre (2oz per square yard) of Growmore ten days before planting. Use a dibber or handfork to set the seedlings 30cm (12in) apart in rows 37.5cm (15in) distant. No matter how moist the site, water them in to settle soil around their roots. Hoe regularly to behead food-stealing weeds, or lay a porous weed-suppressing membrane. As the stem base swells, cut off older, fading leaves and remove competing side shoots.

Feeding
Water copiously in dry periods to avoid any check to growth. In early summer, apply 28g per sq m (1oz per sq yd) of Nitro-Chalk and hoe it shallowly into the root area.

Problems
Control celery leaf miner larvae, which feed between upper and lower leaf surfaces and blister leaves, by removing affected leaves and putting them in the bin. Tackle celery leaf spot, which causes brown spots to appear, by dosing plants with carbendazim when the disease appears. Beat slugs by scattering blue slug pellets.

HARVESTING

Lifting
Prise up globes with a fork in October, trim off roots and cut back leaves to 5cm (2in) from the base. Store globes with leaf stumps showing, in boxes of sand or sawdust, in a dry, airy, frost-free place. In mild areas, leave plants *in situ* and cut back leaves. Cover rows with a thick layer of straw.

CELERIAC AT A GLANCE

A biennial enjoyed for its celery-flavoured bulbous stem bases in autumn and winter.

		RECOMMENDED VARIETIES
JAN	/	
FEB	sow	
MAR	sow	'Alabaster'
APR	sow	'Brilliant'
MAY	transplant	'Iram'
JUN	transplant	'Monarch'
JULY	/	'Snevhide'
AUG	/	'Snow White'
SEPT	/	
OCT	harvest	
NOV	harvest	
DEC	harvest	

CELERY
Apium graveolens

SELF-BLANCHING CELERY is best grown in a block, enclosed by boards. Set plants closely on heavily manured soil for crisp sticks.

FEATURES

Celery forms a tight collection of green stalks or stems to 25cm (10in) tall, topped with many divided leaves. There are trench varieties, which are blanched by mounding soil over their stems, and self-blanching kinds that are grown in a block to ensure succulent sticks. Stalks, leaves and seeds are edible. Blanched sticks of trench celery can be grown by covering stalks with opaque coverings fixed with string. Stalks are also gradually earthed up as they grow. Leaves should be left exposed to sunlight.

CONDITIONS

Aspect
Site
Prefers full sun but will tolerate light shade. Soil needs to be neutral to alkaline. Liming will reduce acidity. Enrich beds with manure or garden compost, adding a complete fertiliser. Monthly side dressings of fertiliser and regular watering are desirable.

GROWING METHOD

Sowing and planting
Raise seedlings in a heated propagator in early spring. Prick out seedlings singly in 7.5cm (3in) pots and harden off for transplanting in late May or early June when frosts finish. Set trench varieties 22.5cm (9in) apart in a single row. Plant self-blanching varieties 22.5cm (9in) apart in a block, to reduce light reaching stems. Further reduce light by enclosing outer rows with boards 30cm (12in) wide. In April, if you are growing trench celery, take out a trench 30cm (12in) deep and 37.5cm (15in) wide. Fork a liberal quantity of manure or spent mushroom compost into the base. Fill in with soil to within 7.5cm (3in) of the top. Blanching trench varieties: In August, when plants are about 30cm (12in) high, remove side shoots and wrap corrugated cardboard loosely around stems and tie it in place. Fill the trench with soil. In late August, mound soil against the stems to exclude light. Finish earthing up in mid September, leaving the leafy tops showing.

Feeding
A feeding programme is necessary to ensure constant, healthy growth. Before planting enrich beds with complete fertiliser. Apply regular dressings of a balanced fertiliser throughout the growing period. An occasional application of sulphate of ammonia will assist growth. Celery requires a great deal of water from seed to maturity, with daily watering being needed during hot dry weather. Lack of water leads to slow growth and stringy, tasteless stalks. As it is a shallow rooting plant, constant watering may result in essential nutrients being leached from the soil.

Problems
Few pests bother celery, but leaf miner may cause blisters to appear. If damage is slight, pick off and burn blistered leaves; if severe, spray with insecticide.

HARVESTING

Picking
Celery matures 30–35 weeks from sowing. Cut whole plant at ground level before seed stalks appear, or occasionally break off outside stems as needed.

CELERY AT A GLANCE		
Grown as annuals in moist, rich soil, self-blanching kinds are planted in a block, and hardy trench varieties are earthed up.		
JAN	harvest	RECOMMENDED VARIETIES
FEB	/	**Self blanching:**
MAR	sow	'Celebrity'
APR	/	'Lathom Self Blanching'
MAY	transplant	'Pink Champagne'
JUN	transplant	'Victoria'
JULY	/	
AUG	harvest	**Trench:**
SEPT	harvest	'Giant Red'
OCT	harvest	'Giant White'
NOV	harvest	'Hopkin's Fenlander'
DEC	harvest	'White Pascal'

CHINESE BROCCOLI

Brassica oleracea var. *alboglabra*

RESEMBLING WESTERN sprouting broccoli and acclaimed for its flowering shoots, Chinese broccoli is sown from late spring to autumn.

FEATURES

Chinese broccoli, also known as Chinese kale, is a stout leafy plant that grows to around 45cm (18in). It has thick, crisp and waxy blue-green to grey leaves. Prized for its flowering shoots, succulent stems and tender young leaves, it resembles a cross between calabrese and purple sprouting broccoli. Chinese broccoli is cultivated for its chunky edible 1–2cm (0.375–0.75in) thick stem. It is only suitable for container growing if young plants are to be harvested. Older plants need to be grown in the garden. It has a small, shallow rooting system, but grows vigorously and matures in around 12–14 weeks. Secondary shoots will appear after the main flowering shoot has been cut.

CONDITIONS

Aspect   Chinese broccoli does best in a sunny position. It should be protected from strong winds which may 'lift' and move the plant as a result of its shallow rooting system. For plants exposed to windy conditions, firm soil up

Site   around stem bases for strength and protection. Grow in fertile, well-drained beds. Fortify the soil with organic material such as well-rotted garden compost or manure.

GROWING METHOD

Sowing and planting   Raise an early crop by sowing in gentle heat in early spring, pricking out seedlings singly in pots, hardening off and transplanting when frosts finish. Set plants 30cm (12in) apart each way. Continue with a main crop sowing outdoors from late spring to early autumn. In chilly gardens, delay sowing until frosts finish, as any check to growth could trigger bolting. For a late crop, sow in late summer or early autumn and move plants under glass in October, to crop throughout winter. If sowing *in situ*, take out drills 1.3cm (0.5in) deep and 30cm (12in) apart and thin seedlings progressively to 30cm (12in) distant. Alternatively, raise plants on a seed bed and transplant seedlings when 7.5cm (3in) tall.

Feeding   As a leafy crop, it grows quickly, so keep soil moist and water frequently. In winter dig in bulky organic matter. Rake in a complete fertiliser ten days before sowing. Apply dressings of sulphate of ammonia periodically through the growing season or give weekly applications of seaweed fertiliser.

Problems   Susceptible to downy mildew. Treat with appropriate fungicide. Guard against slugs and caterpillars.

HARVESTING

Picking   If plant is left to mature, it can be harvested over a long period. Cut the shoots or stems when they are approximately 15cm (6in) long and before the flowers open. Alternatively, the whole plant can be harvested while quite young, usually about 6 weeks after sowing.

CHINESE BROCCOLI AT A GLANCE

A stocky brassica, similar to sprouting broccoli, yielding succulent flowering shoots from summer to winter.

		RECOMMENDED VARIETIES
JAN	/	F1 'Green Lance'
FEB	/	
MAR	sow	
APR	sow transplant	
MAY	sow	
JUN	sow harvest	
JULY	sow harvest	
AUG	sow harvest	
SEPT	sow	
OCT	transplant	
NOV	/	
DEC	harvest	

CHINESE CABBAGE
Brassica rapa var. pekinensis

WONDERFUL SHREDDED in salads – Chinese cabbage plants are raised in sun-warmed soil to avoid any check to growth.

FEATURES

Chinese cabbage has many names including celery cabbage and wong bok. It has wide, thick, crisp leaves with a prominent, broad-based midrib. The upright heads are either loose or tight, depending on variety. Leaf colour varies between dark and light green with inner leaves having a creamy-white colour. Chinese cabbage grows to 20–25cm (8–10in). Flavour ranges from mustardy to sweet and is rather like a lettuce. It is not suitable for growing in containers.

CONDITIONS

Aspect Prefers an open sunny position but tolerates partial shade. Shelter from cold winds and frost.

Site Deep, well-drained soils, high in organic matter will retain soil moisture and lessen soil compaction. Avoid both light and heavy soils and lime if necessary so that the pH is 6.5–7.

GROWING METHOD

Sowing and planting Enjoy a succession of heads by making three main sowings: in gentle heat from late spring to early summer; *in situ* outdoors from early to late summer; in modules in late summer.
First sowing: Avoid any check to growth,

which can cause plants to run to seed, by setting 2 or 3 seeds per small peat pot. Thin seedlings to the one strongest per pot. Harden off and transplant when frosts finish. Set plants in cloche-warmed soil, 30cm (12in) apart.
Second sowing: Take out drills 1.3cm (0.5in) deep and 30cm (12in) apart and sow thinly. Thin seedlings progressively to 30cm (12in) apart.
Third sowing: Sow in modules (peat pots, etc) and transplant sturdy seedlings into an unheated greenhouse in September.
Rapid growth results from regular feeding and watering. Slow growth leads to plants bolting to seed, especially in hot, dry weather. Mulch heavily to retain soil moisture and encourage robust growth. Tie heads loosely with string as heads mature to increase volume of tender white leaves.

Feeding In winter, incorporate bulky organic matter. Before planting rake in a complete fertiliser such as blood, fish and bone meal. When seedlings are 5cm (2in) high apply a further dressing of the same fertiliser and water in immediately. When cabbages start to form heads, feed again. This shallow-rooting vegetable requires a great deal of watering to encourage fast growth. Irrigation between beds helps keep water off leaves and reduces risk of fungal diseases.

Problems Protect Chinese cabbage from club root by liming, and rotate with an unrelated crop over a few years. Use insecticidal sprays against caterpillars and aphids.

HARVESTING

Picking This quick growing crop matures in 10–12 weeks from sowing and should be cropped when weather conditions are dry. Timing is essential as the appearance of seed stalks will cause heads to split. When ready, cut heads just above soil level.

CHINESE CABBAGE AT A GLANCE

Large and succulent cos-lettuce-like heads. Grow them fast and unchecked in warm, fertile soil. Protect from slugs.

Month	Activity		Recommended Varieties
Jan	/		
Feb	/		F1 'Kasumi'
Mar	sow		F1 'Monument'
Apr	sow, transplant		'Orange Queen'
May	transplant		F1 'Ruffles'
Jun	sow		F1 'Tiptop'
July	sow	harvest	
Aug	sow	harvest	
Sept	harvest		
Oct	harvest		
Nov	harvest		
Dec	harvest		

COURGETTE
Cucurbita pepo

THE COURGETTE FRUIT *develops from the base of the yellow flower. This attractive plant will also do well in containers.*

FEATURES

Courgettes are actually marrows (see page 44), picked when quite young. They grow on bushes, are prolific and are ideal for container growing. The vegetable is elongated in shape (although tear-shaped and round varieties exist) and dark green through to yellow. They are best cut when 10–15cm (4–6in) long. Young fruits may be sliced and eaten raw in salads; older ones are delicious cooked.

CONDITIONS

Aspect   Can be grown in full sun to partial shade but needs shelter from cold winds.

Site   Tolerates a wide range of soils, but good drainage is essential. It's a heavy feeder and benefits from heavily fertilised soil, so dig in plenty of well-rotted manure and compost several weeks ahead of planting.

GROWING METHOD

Sowing and planting   For an early crop, raise plants in gentle heat in late April. Set seeds on edge, 1.3cm (0.5in) deep, in small pots of multipurpose compost and germinate them in a temperature of 19°C. Plant one seed per pot to avoid competition. Ideally, grow them in peat pots so that when you transplant them, pot and all, there is no check to growth. Harden off and transplant outdoors when frosts finish in early June. Alternatively, sow outdoors in late May or early June. Take out planting holes 30cm (12in) deep and wide and fill them to within 15cm (6in) of the rim with old manure forked into the base. Cover with soil. Work blood, fish and bone meal or a balanced chemical fertiliser into the top 15cm (6in). Sow three seeds 2.5cm (1in) deep and thin to the one strongest seedling. Space planting stations 60cm (2ft) apart each way. Plants may also be raised in growing bags or pots on a sunny patio. Keep areas around bushes free of weeds and other decaying matter which might harbour disease. Cultivate only lightly, trying not to disturb the delicate root structure. If no fruit develops it may be because cold weather has reduced bee activity around flowers. Overcome by hand-pollinating female flowers. All you do is remove a fully-formed male flower, strip off the petals and dab pollen on to the sticky stigma of a female flower to fertilise it.

Feeding   Rake in a complete fertiliser just before sowing. Liquid feed weekly with a high potash fertiliser when first fruits start to swell. However, remember that too much fertiliser will promote vigorous green growth at the expense of fruit development. Keep water off stems and foliage, especially when fruit is setting. Sandy soils need more water than heavy ones. Lack of water may cause partly-formed fruit to fall. Leaves wilt during hot weather but recover if soil is kept moist.

Problems   Powdery mildew and bacterial wilt are common. Preventative care is important. Do not handle plants while wet and maintain garden hygiene. Control aphids affecting soft growth by spraying with insecticide. If fruits wither after setting, it is probable that bad drainage, causing poor root development, is responsible. Overcome the problem by working grit and organic matter into the soil to open it up and improve air circulation.

HARVESTING

Picking   Gather the fruits when they are 10–15cm (4–6in) long and the skin is soft. Frequent cutting will prolong production.

COURGETTE AT A GLANCE

Romping in full sun on a manured site, courgettes (immature marrows) are harvested from summer to early autumn.

Month	Activity		Recommended Varieties
JAN	/		'Ambassador'
FEB	/		'Bambino'
MAR	/		'Elite'
APR	sow		F1 'Green Bush'
MAY	sow		'Gold Rush'
JUN	sow, transplant		F1 'Zucchini'
JULY	harvest		
AUG	harvest		
SEPT	harvest		
OCT	/		
NOV	/		
DEC	/		

CUCUMBER
Cucumis sativus

TRAILING CUCUMBERS need plenty of space and are not suitable for containers. This variety, with its attractive bright yellow flowers, has been placed at the back of the garden against a supporting wire fence. Bush varieties, taking up less space, are better for smaller plots.

FEATURES

Bush and trailing varieties of outdoor and greenhouse cucumber come in many forms – varying from long or short and green, to round and whitish like an apple. An easily digestible, thin-skinned bush variety, 'Burpless Tasty Green', has become very popular. Never interplant standard (ordinary) varieties with all-female types, for if the odd male flower is left on the plant it will pollinate the all-female varieties and cause the fruits to become bulbous and bitter. Greenhouse cucumbers need more humidity than tomatoes, which should have a drier atmosphere. However, in practice, the two can be successfully grown together.

CONDITIONS

Aspect Outdoor (ridge) varieties need a warm, sunny spot sheltered from cold winds. Greenhouse kinds, as the name implies, are best grown under glass.

Site To save space, outdoor trailing varieties can be trained up a supporting trellis, resulting in cleaner, better-formed fruit than those grown on the ground. Beds need to be enriched with rotted garden compost or manure. Adding lime to acid soils in high rainfall areas will

reduce risk of molybdenum trace element deficiency. This deficiency is recognised by mottling or yellowing and upward curling of leaves. Spraying young plants with a solution of sodium molybdate, 5g (0.2oz) to 5 litres (10 pints) water, will rectify this deficiency. Mulch soils heavily to avoid compaction and to compensate for the heavy watering cycle which is essential for the successful growth of cucumbers.

CUCUMBER AT A GLANCE

Trailing, frost-tender plants grown in a greenhouse, frame or outdoors. Cut fruits regularly to ensure a lengthy succession.

			RECOMMENDED VARIETIES
JAN	/		
FEB	sow		**Greenhouse (all-female):**
MAR	transplant		F1 'Aidas'
APR	sow		F1 'Carmen'
MAY	sow, transplant		F1 'Danimas'
JUN	sow, transplant		F1 'Petita'
JULY	harvest		**Ridge:**
AUG	harvest		'Bush Champion'
SEPT	harvest		F1 'Burpless Tasty Green'
OCT	/		F1 'Jazzer'
NOV	/		'Marketmore'
DEC	/		

ALL-FEMALE VARIETIES OF GREENHOUSE CUCUMBER are prolific and easy to care for. Unlike standard varieties, they don't bear male flowers. If the male flowers of standard varieties pollinate female blooms, it causes fruits to distort.

GROWING METHOD

Sowing and planting

For planting in a well-heated greenhouse in early spring, sow seeds – one per small pot – edgewise and 1.3cm (0.5in) deep. Germinate in a heated propagator (at 16°C for male and female varieties or 21°C for all-female varieties) in late February or early March.

For planting in an unheated greenhouse in late May, sow seeds in a heated propagator in late April.

For planting outdoors, raise seedlings in gentle heat in late April or sow *in situ* outdoors in late May or early June in manure- and fertiliser-enriched planting holes 45cm (18in) apart. Grow trailing kinds as decorative plants to scramble over trellis, screens, wire fences, or even into open-headed, bushy trees. They have great appeal when clothing an arch or pergola. Both bush and trailing varieties prosper in growing bags, especially if you site them against a brick wall that absorbs heat by day and releases it at night. Cucumbers also do well when grown on top of compost heaps. But before sowing or planting, take out a good depth of unrotted waste and refill the hole with fertile topsoil.

Greenhouse plants: Aim at maintaining a minimum temperature of 16°C for ordinary varieties, or 10 degrees higher for all-female kinds. When setting plants, one to a 22.5cm (9in) pot or two to a standard sized growing bag, make sure their necks are slightly above the compost to reduce risk of neck rot.

Water freely and spray pots, staging and floor with water to maintain high a level of humidity. Support stem with a cane and tie it to horizontal wires. Pinch out side shoots bearing embryo cucumbers, two leaves beyond the fruit. Nip out flowerless stems when 60cm (2ft) long.

Outdoor plants: Pinch out shoot tips when six or seven leaves have formed, to encourage side shoots to develop. Ideally, cover plants with individual cloches or grow them under tunnel cloches.

Feeding

Cucumbers have an extremely high water content so plants need to be kept moist when growing vigorously. Feed weekly with a high potash liquid fertiliser when first fruits start to swell.

Problems

Aphids and red spider mite will need to be sprayed with insecticide if natural predators, which control them biologically, cannot cope. Powdery mildew is a common disease which discolours leaves. Spraying with carbendazim-based fungicide is normally successful.

HARVESTING

Picking

Greenhouse fruits: Gather fruits when 15–20cm (6–8in) long. Don't let them become fat and old, as this will halt production.

Outdoor fruits: Cut them when about 15cm (6in) long; apple varieties should not be larger than a small orange.

In both instances, seeds should be small and immature.

ENDIVE
Cichorium endivia

BLANCH curly- and plain-leaved endive by loosely tying up leaves and covering head with a flower pot with blocked drainage holes.

FEATURES

This salad vegetable is similar to lettuce but with chewier and more substantial, slightly bitter leaves. There are two frequently-grown forms: green curly endive which has a loose head, finely serrated or frilly leaf edges and white midribs, and Batavian endive which has broad, thick leaves that are smooth and light green.

CONDITIONS

Aspect Prefers bright sunlight. In hot weather it may be necessary to shade seedlings.

Site Make sure the bed has good drainage and has previously been well worked and manured. The rooting system of endive is shallow, so there needs to be food close to the surface. Dig manure into the top 20cm (8in) of soil. Endive prefers neutral to slighly acid soils, with a pH range of 6–7.

GROWING METHOD

Sowing and planting Sow seeds in prepared soil from late March to early September for harvesting succulent hearts from August to February. Take out seed drills 1.3cm (0.5in) deep and 30cm (12in) apart, and sow the seeds thinly. Thin seedlings of curly leaved varieties at intervals, to 22.5cm (9in) apart, and plain or broad-leaved varieties to 30cm (12in) apart. Mulch around the plants with straw, leaves or grass clippings, or other bulky organics, to keep roots cool and moist. This also helps to keep down weeds. Endive will sometimes grow back after cropping, but the quality is usually not good. It is best to treat endive as an annual and to sow every year.

Feeding Prepare the garden beds for growing endives by digging in old manure or rotted garden compost. Two weeks before sowing, rake in a balanced fertiliser. Water endive regularly to encourage rapid growth. Overhead sprinklers are not recommended as surplus water becomes trapped inside the endive head, which can cause it to rot.

Problems Endive has no serious problems, but control slugs and snails with a molluscicide, or organically by sinking deep saucers of stale beer in the ground, with the rim slightly above soil level, to attract and drown these pests. Beat aphids, which may colonise soft leaves, by spraying with a pirimicarb-based insecticide.

HARVESTING

Picking If the very young leaves are not cropped, endive will reach maturity in three months. Unblanched leaves are bitter, so whiten them about 12 weeks after sowing. When conditions are dry, tie in the leaves with raffia and cover the hearts with flower pots, the drainage holes of which have been blocked to exclude light. This exclusion of sunlight, or blanching, slows down the production of chlorophyll (green colouring) in the leaves and whitens and sweetens them. Blanch just a few heads at a time.

ENDIVE AT A GLANCE

A member of the chicory family, its plump green, plain or curly leaved heads are blanched to remove the bitter taste.

		RECOMMENDED VARIETIES
JAN	harvest	**Plain-leaved:**
FEB	harvest	'Golda'
MAR	sow	
APR	sow	**Curly-leaved:**
MAY	sow	'Ione'
JUN	sow	'Sally'
JULY	sow	'Tres Fine Maraichere'
AUG	sow harvest	(Coquette)
SEPT	sow harvest	'Green Moss Curled'
OCT	harvest	
NOV	harvest	
DEC	harvest	

FLORENCE FENNEL

Foeniculum vulgare dulce

ENCOURAGE THE ANISEED-FLAVOURED stem base to swell quickly to cricket ball size by watering copiously, liquid feeding and mounding soil over it.

CLOSELY-RELATED – common fennel. Use chopped leaves to flavour fish and salads.

FEATURES

A perennial grown as an annual, the large swollen and aniseed-flavoured leaf base of Florence fennel forms quickly in warm soil. Serve the foliage and the bulbous base in salads, or boil the 'bulb' for 30–40 minutes, drain and mantle with melted butter or cheese sauce. Florence fennel has two widely grown relations – the feathery, green-leaved herb, common fennel (*Foeniculum vulgare*), and its purple-leaved form (*F. vulgare 'Purpureum'*). Both add piquancy to fish dishes. Small yellow flowers clustered in umbels appear during the summer and produce small oval-shaped, ribbed brown seeds.

CONDITIONS

Aspect Must have warmth and plenty of sun. Plant fennel towards the back of garden where it will be a good backdrop for other plants. The feathery leaves may require tying and support against strong wind.

Site Both common and Florence fennel will grow in most soils (pH range of 6–7 preferred) but it is advisable to dig in plenty of compost and well-rotted animal manure and have well-drained beds. Applications of lime are needed if the soil is very acid.

GROWING METHODS

Sowing and planting Florence fennel is best grown in rows across a sunny plot. It hates root disturbance, so is best sown *in situ* from May to early July. Take out seed drills 1.3cm (0.5in) deep and 45cm (18in) apart and set seeds thinly. Firm soil over them. Water freely if soil is dry. When seedlings are 2.5cm (1in) high, thin them to 30cm (12in) apart. Cover plants with cloches if weather turns chilly. Mulch to keep roots cool and moist and, when the stem bases start to swell, mound soil over them to blanch and sweeten them.

Problems Florence fennel has no specific pest or disease problems.

HARVESTING

Cutting Cut the swollen, aniseed-flavoured base of Florence fennel when it reaches the size of a tennis ball – which is generally from August to September.

FLORENCE FENNEL AT A GLANCE

Sown in warm soil in mid spring, plants develop bulbous-based stems which are harvested from late summer to autumn.

Month		RECOMMENDED VARIETIES
JAN	/	
FEB	/	
MAR	/	'Sweet Florence'
APR	/	'Cantino'
MAY	sow	F1 'Rudy'
JUN	/	'Sirio'
JULY	/	' Zefa Fino'
AUG	harvest	
SEPT	harvest	
OCT	harvest	
NOV	/	
DEC	/	

FRENCH BEAN

Phaseolus vulgaris

FRENCH BEANS, unlike runner beans, are self-fertile, and are not dependent on insect pollination.

FEATURES

The French bean is a South American half-hardy annual. Bush and climbing varieties yield slender, succulent pods from late June to October. Being self-fertile, it's an excellent substitute for runner beans in hot dry summers when bees have difficulty entering and pollinating the runners' deflated blooms. Pods are flat or cylindrical and yellow, green, purple or streaked. They are picked and eaten fresh or seeds are allowed to mature and shelled and stored for winter.

CONDITIONS

Aspect
Site

A sunny spot sheltered from damaging wind. Grow French beans on light, freely draining, neutral to slightly acid loam that was well manured the previous autumn. Raise the pH of acid soil by raking in lime in autumn or winter. Avoid heavy clay in which roots may rot.

GROWING METHOD

Sowing and planting

Early sowings under cloches in early April will be ready for picking in late June. Follow with successional unprotected sowings from May, when nights are warming. Finish with a July sowing, cloched in mid September, for gathering in autumn. If you garden in a cold district seeds won't germinate until the soil temperature has risen to 12°C. Gain a head start by germinating seeds in a greenhouse. Set them singly in small peat pots and transplant hardened-off seedlings outdoors when 5–7.5cm (2–3in) high.

Bush varieties:

Take out drills 5cm (2in) deep and 45cm (18in) apart and set seeds 10cm (4in) apart. Firm soil over them. Sow a few seeds at the end of the row for 'gapping up' failures. Prop up stems to keep pods away from slugs.

Climbing varieties:

Before sowing, erect a double row of 2.4m (8ft) criss-crossed canes 60cm (2ft) apart. Space canes 15cm (6in) apart along the row and tie them to horizontal cross members positioned 60cm (2ft) from the top. Alternatively, arrange canes as a wigwam or train plants over tensioned bean netting secured to a braced wood or metal frame. Set one seed 5cm (2in) deep beside each cane, or 15cm (6in) apart if growing plants up netting. Hoe regularly to control weeds.

Feeding

Rake in a balanced fertiliser 10 days before sowing and apply a high potash liquid fertiliser fortnightly in summer. Water freely when flowers appear, but not beforehand unless it is very dry, for excessive moisture may trigger more foliage than blooms.

Problems

Fairly trouble free. Control sap-sucking green or black aphids that colonise shoot tips and leaf undersides by spraying with insecticide when pests are seen. Grey mould, which coats developing pods in damp, humid weather, is best tackled by spraying with carbendazim when flowers are forming.

HARVESTING

Picking

Pick pods – a single plant will crop for about 5–7 weeks – when 10–15cm (4–6in) long, two or three times a week. Never let pods grow old, for they will halt production. Roots are shallow, so hold the plant when picking to avoid loosening it. Gather dried (haricot) beans in autumn when the pods are straw coloured. Dry seeds on newspaper for several days before storing them in airtight jars.

FRENCH BEANS AT A GLANCE

A frost-tender annual prized for a succession of slender, succulent pods from spring to autumn.

		RECOMMENDED VARIETIES
JAN	/	**Bush:**
FEB	/	'Ferrari'
MAR	/	'Copper Teepee'
APR	sow	'Lasso'
MAY	sow	'Saffron'
JUN	sow / harvest	'Brown Dutch' (haricot type)
JULY	harvest	
AUG	harvest	
SEPT	harvest	**Climbing:**
OCT	/	'Blue Lake'
NOV	/	'Hunter'
DEC	/	'Violet Podded'

GARLIC
Allium sativum

PLANT GARLIC cloves on a sunny, fertile and well-drained patch from early to late autumn. Lift bulbs when leaves turn yellow.

FEATURES

A bulbous perennial (although usually grown as an annual), garlic has green, curved, flat, spear-like leaves and grows to 60–90cm (2–3ft) high. Cloves, sheathed in a papery covering, are compacted to form a bulb and cling to a central stem. They have a strong odour and taste. The plant has a central rounded stalk in summer with a large rounded flower head composed of numerous pinkish-white petals.

CONDITIONS

Aspect Prefers full sun in an open position.
Site Soil should be well-drained sandy loam, rich in humus and limy. Raise the pH of strongly acid soils by applying 112g per square metre (4oz per square yard) of Dolomite limestone. Keep weed-free. If your soil is heavy clay, grow plants on ridges to ensure that surplus moisture drains from the root system. Additionally, fork in sharp sand, bonfire ash or crumbly garden compost to improve aeration further. Alternatively, grow your garlic plants in raised beds.

GROWING METHOD

Planting Plant cloves, which should be about 1.3cm (0.5in) across and about 10g (0.3oz) in weight, in late October or November, as plant requires a cold spell (0–10°C) for one or two months. If soil is too heavy, defer planting until early spring. Set cloves, split from the bulb, directly into the ground where the plants are to grow, 15cm (6in) apart in rows and 2.5cm (1in) deep. Rows should be 30cm (12in) apart. Make sure that you plant the cloves the right way up – it's not always obvious – by making sure that the flattish 'base plate' is at the bottom.

Feeding Do not enrich soil with manure unless the manure is completely broken down. If used, work in several months before planting. Keep soil damp but not overwet. Water sparingly when bulbs mature, making sure surplus moisture draws away freely otherwise the bulbs will not store satisfactorily.

Problems Garlic is usually trouble free as the strong oils and chemicals in its foliage repel insects. It also has antiseptic properties which deter bacteria and fungal diseases. Keep plants well spaced to reduce humidity which can adversely affect the plant, especially in coastal areas. Garlic is useful as a companion plant for fruit trees, tomatoes and roses. Strong secretions of sulphur from garlic are thought to improve the scent of roses.

HARVESTING

Picking Harvest the bulbs when the leaves begin to turn yellow in mid summer. Ripen them off in a sunny spot, ideally on netting raised on a frame of canes, and cover them if rain threatens. When the necks are crisp and dry, rope the bulbs and store them in a temperature of 5–10°C. They must be kept dry. Bulbs will keep well for up to ten months.

GARLIC AT A GLANCE

A hardy perennial, treated as an annual, grown for its strongly flavoured cloves which add piquancy to salad and cooked dishes.

Month	Activity		Recommended Varieties
Jan	/		
Feb	plant	🌰	'Longkeeper'
Mar	plant	🌰	'Mersley White'
Apr	/		
May	/		
Jun	/		
July	harvest	🌱	
Aug	harvest	🌱	
Sept	harvest	🌱	
Oct	plant	🌰	
Nov	plant	🌰	
Dec	/		

GLOBE ARTICHOKE
Cynara scolymus

SUCCULENT FLOWER BUDS are ready for eating when green and swollen but before scales open.

GROWN IN A BORDER, globe artichoke's large sculptural flowers and silver leaves associate well with red, purple and yellow blooms.

FEATURES

Globe artichoke is a grey-green perennial 1.2–1.5m (4–5ft) tall with decorative compound leaves resembling those of the Scotch thistle. Edible parts are the young, tender, globe-shaped flower buds which are harvested and eaten before opening. This attractive plant requires plenty of space. The plant is not only good to eat, but also makes a splendid statement at the back of a border.

CONDITIONS

Aspect Best grown in areas with mild, relatively frost-free winters and damp cool summers. Prefers full sunlight.

Site Grow in rich, well-drained soils. Prepare beds by digging in crumbly manure or compost in autumn.

GLOBE ARTICHOKE AT A GLANCE

A perennial that is just hardy, it is enjoyed for its succulent, thistle-like flower buds that are produced in summer.

Jan	/	RECOMMENDED VARIETIES
Feb	sow, plant	'Green Globe'
Mar	sow, plant	
Apr	/	
May	/	
Jun	harvest	
July	harvest	
Aug	harvest	
Sept	harvest	
Oct	/	
Nov	/	
Dec	/	

GROWING METHOD

Sowing and planting For best results obtain rooted shoots (suckers) from specialist nurseries. Success from seed is variable and it takes approximately one year from sowing to harvesting. Ideally, plant in spring. As artichokes require plenty of space, set plants 1m (3ft) apart each way. Hoe to keep down weeds. In autumn when leaves start dying, cut back stems to 15cm (6in) from the base and cover crowns with leaves, bracken or straw. Remove this frost-insulating material in spring. Divide mature plants in early spring every third year. Reset healthy young divisions in manured soil.

Feeding Fortify the soil before planting by raking in 56g per sq m (2oz per sq yd) of balanced fertiliser. Apply a further dressing around plants in mid summer. Liquid feed with high potash fertiliser if growth is slow. Water freely after planting and mulch the root area thickly with crumbly organic material. Keep soil evenly and constantly moist, carefully monitoring this throughout the spring and summer months.

Problems Good drainage is essential otherwise crown rot may develop, principally as a result of the heavy mulching. Handle plants as little as possible and remove any infected or diseased specimens immediately.

HARVESTING

Picking After planting suckers in spring, artichokes take 2–3 months to reach maturity. In most areas, harvesting takes place from mid to late summer when buds are tight and about 8cm (3in) across. Cut well below the bud with 2.5cm (1in) of stem still attached. The optimum bearing period is the second year after planting.

JERUSALEM ARTICHOKE

Helianthus tuberosus

JERUSALEM ARTICHOKES are so often planted across one end of the plot, to produce a weighty crop of nutritious, starch-free tubers.

FEATURES

A very hardy perennial belonging to the sunflower family, it produces edible tubers resembling young, gnarled potatoes. Rather sweet to taste, Jerusalem artichokes can be cooked in much the same way as potatoes: roasted, boiled or pureed in soups. It is not related to the globe artichoke. Above ground, the plant can grow to 2.1m (7ft) and produces attractive, dark-centred, yellow flowers with small seeds.

CONDITIONS

Aspect   Prefers a sunny position but will tolerate light shade. Requires staking on a windy plot.

Site   Prefers a well-drained soil. Bigger tubers will result if the bed is well prepared in autumn or winter before planting. Dig in plenty of organic matter. Add a little lime and balanced fertiliser just before planting. Water sparingly.

GROWING METHOD

Sowing and planting   Plant tubers from late winter to mid-spring. Set them 45cm (18in) apart and 15cm (6in) deep in furrows 90cm (3ft) apart. As, normally, only a single row is grown, for the crop casts much shade, it is sited at the end of the plot to act as a windbreak. Ridge soil lightly over rows. When plants are about 30cm (12in) high, use a draw hoe to mound soil around stem bases. When plants are 90–120cm (3–4ft) high, tie them to a tensioned wire fixed to two braced posts. The young shoots are at their most vulnerable in summer, so guard against snails and slugs. To improve tuber quality, nip out flowerheads at bud stage. In autumn, just before harvesting, cut back tall flower stems close to the ground. In cold districts cover stem bases with straw, leaves or fibre fleece to insulate the roots from hard frosts.

Feeding   Spur robust growth by liquid feeding weekly with a high potash fertiliser from spring to late summer. Do not overwater, but keep soil moist during dry spells.

Problems   Snails and slugs may appear as shoots form. Use molluscicides to control them or trap them in small containers of stale beer sunk to just above soil level. (This prevents ground beetles falling in and drowning.)

HARVESTING

Lifting   In October, when growth is dying back and leaves are turning brown, lift tubers, as required, until early spring. Save a few tubers at the end of the season for planting new rows in late winter. Make sure you have removed all tubers from the soil, as any remaining will appear as weeds and may disrupt other crops.

JERUSALEM ARTICHOKE AT A GLANCE

A tall, leafy crop, often planted as a wind break, it yields nutritious and tasty, starch-free tubers that are dug like potatoes.

Month	Activity		RECOMMENDED VARIETIES
JAN	harvest		
FEB	plant		'Common'
MAR	plant		'Sunray Dwarf'
APR	plant		'Fuseau'
MAY	/		
JUN	/		
JULY	/		
AUG	/		
SEPT	/		
OCT	harvest		
NOV	harvest		
DEC	harvest		

KALE

Brassica oleracea – Acephala group

PRIZED FOR succulent and tasty leaves and shoots, weather-defiant kale is a boon for filling hungry-gap months from winter to early spring.

FEATURES

An exceptionally hardy and very healthy biennial. Varieties range in size from 30cm (12in) to 90cm (3ft) high. Making leafy plants with stocky stems, the tasty side shoots and tender leaves are gathered from November to April. Leaf shapes and textures vary from finely curled and large and plain to 'Ragged Jack' with fringed and reddish leaves. Rape kales – 'Hungry Gap' among them – are sown *in situ* and left to mature there. Other kinds are raised on a seed bed and transplanted.

Usefully, kale, unlike other brassicas, is seldom troubled by club root and cabbage root fly.

KALE AT A GLANCE

A hardy, robust biennial yielding tasty shoots and leaves from winter to spring.

		RECOMMENDED VARIETIES
JAN	harvest	'Dwarf Green Curled'
FEB	harvest	'Hungry Gap' (rape kale)
MAR	harvest	'Nero di Toscana'
APR	sow	'Pentland Brig'
MAY	sow	'Thousand Head'
JUN	transplant	
JULY	transplant	
AUG	/	
SEPT	/	
OCT	harvest	
NOV	harvest	
DEC	harvest	

CONDITIONS

Aspect — Though more weather resistant than other brassicas and thriving in chilly districts, kale is more productive if it is sheltered from icy winds.

Site — Though not fussy about soil, highest yields are won on an open, sunny plot of free-draining but moisture-retentive loam in full sun. Sweeten acid, sandy soil by applying garden lime in November. Enrich poor sites by digging in bulky organic materials, such as old manure or mushroom compost, in the autumn or winter.

GROWING METHOD

Sowing and planting — If you are growing varieties such as 'Dwarf Green Curled', 'Pentland Brig' or 'Nero di Toscana' that are raised on a seed bed in April or May before transplanting to final positions, prepare the ground by raking a fertilised patch of soil to a crumbly tilth. Use the point of a draw hoe, guided by a tensioned garden line, to take out seed drills 1.3cm (0.5in) deep and 15cm (6in) apart. Sow thinly. Cover seeds and use the back of a rake to firm soil. From late June to early August, when seedlings are 10–15cm (4–6in) high, water liberally, lift them with a fork and use a dibber to transplant them 45cm (18in) apart each way. Reduce spacing between dwarf varieties to 37.5cm (15in). Should you opt for 'Hungry Gap' and other varieties that are sown direct, that is, in their cropping positions, take out drills 45cm (18in) apart. For these you should sow very thinly and progressively and space out seedlings to 45cm (18in) apart. Alternatively, set clusters of three seeds 45cm (18in) apart and thin seedlings to the strongest per station. On windy plots, mound soil around the stem base to encourage extra, anchoring roots. It may be advisable to tie each plant to a sturdy cane.

Feeding — Help plants resist hard, shoot-burning frost by sprinkling 28g per sq m (1oz per sq yd) of sulphate of potash over the root area in summer. Water it in if the soil is dry.

Problems — Though club root and cabbage root fly aren't troublesome on kale, aphids can be a problem. Tackle them with a systemic insecticide, such as heptenophos, or partially systemic pirimicarb.

HARVESTING

Picking — Gather succulent leaves and shoots. Pick a few from each plant in turn, from the top downwards, and pull off and discard old, tough, yellowing leaves. Some varieties, such as 'Pentland Brig', produce a succession of shoots over many weeks.

KOHL RABI

Brassica oleracea Gongyloides group

PULL 'BULBS' when sweet and tender and midway between golf and tennis ball size. Enjoy them shredded or sliced in salads.

FEATURES

Kohl, the German word for cabbage, and *rabi,* meaning turnip, perfectly describe kohl rabi. Its cabbage head tops a swollen white, purple or green, turnip-shaped stem. A rosette of edible green leaves grows from the stem base. The flavour lies somewhere between a cabbage and a turnip, but is slightly sweeter than each. It makes an excellent turnip substitute for light, sandy soils in which the crop is seldom successful. Enjoy it raw in salads, or cook it and add to soups and stews.

CONDITIONS

Aspect Prefers sunny beds.
Site Soil should be well drained, cool and moist. Dig in plenty of well-rotted manure in autumn or winter to help conserve moisture in summer.

GROWING METHOD

Sowing Kohl rabi does not transplant readily, so it is preferable to sow seeds *in situ*. Set seeds thinly in drills 1.3cm (0.5in) deep and 30cm (12in) apart. Sow green and white varieties from March to June for pulling in summer; set purple varieties from July to August for harvesting in autumn or winter.

Thin seedlings to 15cm (6in) apart when 5cm (2in) high. Aim for a pH range of 6.5–7.5. Like other brassicas, kohl rabi has a shallow root system, so hoe carefully when weeding. If garden space is limited, set seeds thinly in growing bags. Water freely to speed growth, and pull out and enjoy overcrowded seedlings when the 'bulbs' are tiny, to allow the remainder to grow to full size.

Feeding Rake in a balanced fertiliser ten days before sowing. If the soil is acid, add 112g per square metre (4oz per square yard) of Dolomitic limestone. Continue with weekly liquid feeds of high potash fertiliser when plants are growing strongly. Keep soil evenly moist at all times otherwise the 'bulb' will become woody.

Problems Common pests are caterpillars of the cabbage moth and cabbage white butterfly. Control by spraying with an insecticide when damage is first seen. Downy mildew is a fungal disease which may attack seedlings. Unless it is checked, leaves turn yellow and shrivel and plant dies. Spray with a fungicide. Yellowing of leaves on older plants may also indicate a magnesium deficiency. Overcome this by watering around plants with a solution of 28g (1oz) magnesium sulphate (Epsom salts) in 4.55 litres (1 gallon) of water.

HARVESTING

Lifting The growing season for this vegetable is short – from 8–12 weeks. Pull plants when the stems are midway between golf ball and cricket ball size. Leave them in the ground and gather as required until December. 'Bulbs' cannot be lifted and stored.

KOHL RABI AT A GLANCE

Enjoyed for its mild, cabbage-cum-turnip flavoured swollen stem bases, which are sliced and added to salads or cooked like turnip.

Month	Activity		RECOMMENDED VARIETIES
JAN	/		'Green Vienna'
FEB	/		'Lanro'
MAR	sow		F1 'Quickstar'
APR	sow		'Purple Vienna'
MAY	sow		'Rowel'
JUN	sow	harvest	F1 'Trero'
JULY	sow	harvest	
AUG	sow	harvest	
SEPT	harvest		
OCT	harvest		
NOV	harvest		
DEC	/		

LEEK

Allium ampeloprasum

HARDY and trouble-free, leeks can be dug as required. If severe frost is forecast, lift a batch, box them in soil and keep under cover.

FEATURES

A relative of the onion, this vegetable has a long white underground stem, slightly bulbous at the root end, and green, strap-like leaves. Most leeks are left to grow to the fully mature state but they are much tastier if cropped earlier. The flesh is thick and mildly onion-flavoured.

CONDITIONS

Aspect   Prefers full sun.
Site   Feed regularly and keep weeds down. Leeks are not too fussy about soil type, but thrive in organically rich soil, manured in autumn.

GROWING METHOD

Sowing and planting   For an early crop, raise seedlings in gentle heat in January or February, prick out 5cm (2in) apart into seed trays and transplant outdoors when 20cm (8in) long. Most plants, however, are raised in a seed bed outdoors from March to April. Take out drills 1.3cm (0.5in) deep and 15cm (6in) apart and sow seeds thinly. Firm soil over seeds. When seedlings are 20cm (8in) high, and pencil thick, move them to their cropping quarters. After shortening leaves, removing a third to reduce transpiration, and cutting back extra long roots, use a dibber to make holes 15cm (6in) deep. Drop a leek into a hole and water it in. Do not fill the hole with soil. Over a period, regular watering will gradually deposit soil around the young leek and cover the roots. If extra-long blanched stems are required, mound soil around the plant. Choose a dry day and take care not to get soil into leaf joints, which will make the stems gritty. Ideally, enclose stems with paper or cardboard collars and continue earthing up until mid autumn. Keep soil cool and encourage robust growth by mulching with well-rotted garden compost or crumbly manure. If you do not have any, lay perforated black plastic between rows. This also helps control weeds.

Feeding   After transplanting, encourage strong growth by top dressing rows with a balanced fertiliser, such as Growmore or blood, fish and bone meal. Additionally, liquid feed with a high potash tomato fertiliser from spring to late summer. Water regularly, as moist, fertile soil encourages strong growth.

Problems   Thankfully, leeks are seldom troubled by pests or diseases. If onion thrips appear, remove them by hosing.

HARVESTING

Lifting   Leeks take a long time to produce large stems – about 30 weeks from seed. Never pull leeks from the ground, as they are liable to break. Always use a spade to lift them. If a hard frost is imminent, dig up a batch and heel the leeks in, in a sheltered spot, to draw upon when rows are 'locked in'. They can be harvested at any stage.

LEEK AT A GLANCE

A hardy biennial grown as an annual for its fat, fleshy and blanched white stem, dug from autumn to spring.

Month	Activity		Recommended Varieties
JAN	sow		**Early (Sept-Nov):**
FEB	sow		'Arial'
MAR	sow		'King Richard'
APR	sow, transplant		
MAY	transplant		**Mid-season (Dec-Feb):**
JUN	transplant		'Musselburgh'
JULY	/		'Lyon'
AUG	/		
SEPT	harvest		**Late (Feb-April):**
OCT	harvest		'Giant Winter'
NOV	harvest		'Yates Empire'
DEC	harvest		

LETTUCE

Lactuca sativa

LETTUCES ROMP to maturity in organically rich soil that stays moist in summer. Harvest when heads are firm when gently pressed.

FEATURES

Lettuce, in greatest demand in summer, comes in many varieties for harvesting throughout the year. Hearts are either compact or loosely arranged, and a light green to reddish-brown. The commonly available crispy-leaved iceberg lettuce is an example of a compacted form. Butterhead (cabbage) and oak leaf varieties have soft, loose leaves, while Cos has strong rigid leaves and a distinctively elongated head. Loose leaf and small varieties grow well in containers and make a decorative display.

CONDITIONS

Aspect
Prefers sun to partial shade. Lettuces do not like excessively hot positions. Protective cloches may be needed to help outdoor varieties mature in winter.

Site
This crop prefers non-acidic soils, enriched with decayed manure. Dig in liberal quantities in autumn or winter. Rake in lime to make acid soils alkaline. Beds should be well drained and weeds kept under control. Mulching helps keep shallow roots cool.

GROWING METHOD

Sowing and planting
Sow from February to September for year-round cropping. Grow plants quickly for best results. If a variety is planted out of season it may run to seed, especially in hot weather. Successional sowings at fortnightly intervals from early spring to mid summer ensure continuity. Avoid sowing during very hot weather as high temperatures inhibit germination. Seeds can be raised in containers for later transplanting, but direct sowing into garden beds is preferred. Sow thinly in drills 1.3cm (0.5in) deep and 15–30cm (6–12in) apart according to variety. If sowing in seed trays, lightly cover with no more than 0.5cm (0.2in) of multipurpose compost. Keep soil moist. Thin seedlings progressively until miniature varieties, such as 'Little Gem', are 15cm (6in) apart, and others are 22.5–30cm (9–12in) apart. Harden off heat-raised seedlings before planting out. Mulch with perforated black plastic.

Feeding
A week or so before sowing outdoors, fortify the bed by raking in a balanced fertiliser. Thereafter, apply another dressing of fertiliser after thinning seedlings, and again when half grown. Water in if the soil is dry. Don't let fertiliser touch the leaves, or it may burn them. Hose it off if necessary. Keep plants evenly moist. Overwatering may cause fungal diseases. Lack of water can reduce the head size, cause bolting in hot weather and can trigger bitterness.

Problems
If aphids appear and slow plant growth, control with insecticide. Downy mildew which causes leaves to become papery and pale brown, is remedied with a fungicide. Dead leaves should be burnt. The general health of plants is improved by keeping them well spaced during the growing period.

HARVESTING

Picking
Lettuce takes 8–14 weeks to reach maturity. Loose leaf lettuce are harvested a few leaves at a time, snapping off mature outer leaves when needed. Gather hearting lettuces when the centre feels nicely firm if you press it gently with the back of your hand. Don't squeeze the head or you will damage the leaves.

LETTUCE AT A GLANCE

Leafy annuals, including butterhead, crisphead, cos and loose-leaf types, sown throughout the year for successional harvesting.

JAN	/	
FEB	sow	
MAR	sow/transplant	
APR	sow	
MAY	sow	
JUN	sow	harvest
JULY	sow	harvest
AUG	sow	harvest
SEPT	sow	harvest
OCT	harvest	
NOV	harvest	
DEC	harvest	

RECOMMENDED VARIETIES

Early spring:
'Winter Density'

Late spring-autumn:
'Little Gem'
'Sherwood'
'Blush'
'Webb's Wonderful'
'Frisby' (loose-leaf)

Autumn-early winter:
'Avoncrisp'

Winter-spring:
'Kelly's' (greenhouse)

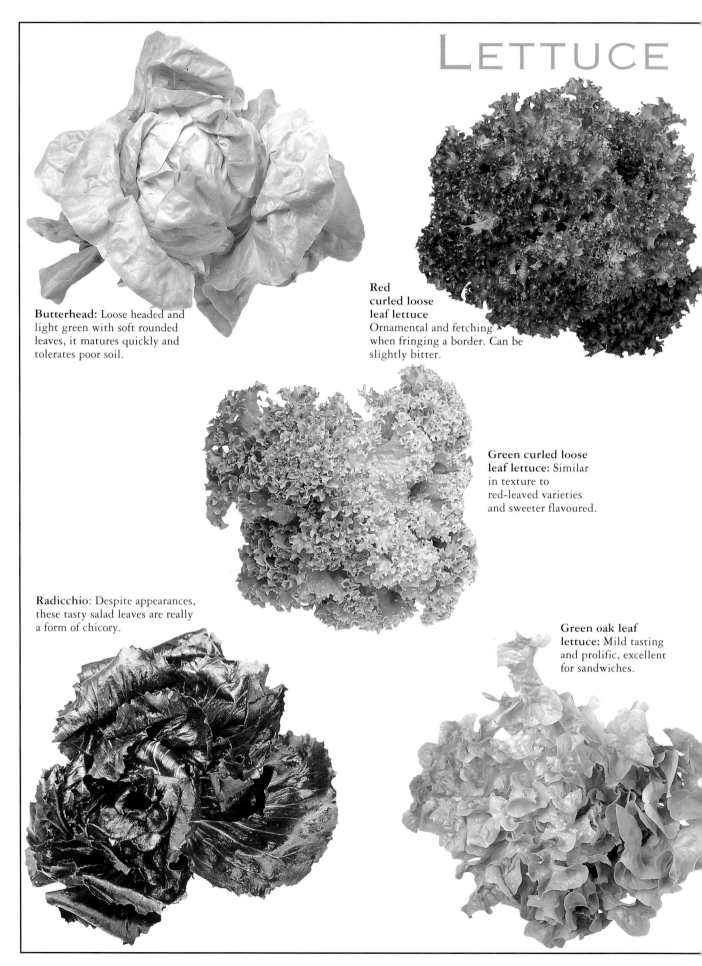

Butterhead: Loose headed and light green with soft rounded leaves, it matures quickly and tolerates poor soil.

Red curled loose leaf lettuce
Ornamental and fetching when fringing a border. Can be slightly bitter.

Green curled loose leaf lettuce: Similar in texture to red-leaved varieties and sweeter flavoured.

Radicchio: Despite appearances, these tasty salad leaves are really a form of chicory.

Green oak leaf lettuce: Mild tasting and prolific, excellent for sandwiches.

VARIETIES

Cos lettuce:
Large, long green heads of crisp, succulent and sweet leaves.

Brown-leaved butterhead:
Red and green leaves with a mild, sweet flavour.

Red oak leaf lettuce: Similar to the green form but with coppery brownish red foliage. Effective when edging a border.

Crisphead, including iceberg varieties: Large, crisp, succulent leaves with a sweet flavour.

MARROW
Cucurbita

ENCOURAGE MARROWS by giving them plenty of manure. Harvest for storage when the skin toughens in September.

FEATURES

Marrows are related to pumpkins and squashes. Courgettes are simply small marrows. Marrows have elongated fruits and the skin colour varies from green, to green and white striped, to white. There is little difference in taste between varieties, although the cooked texture of the flesh varies. Marrow flowers or blossoms are often picked and eaten along with the immature fruit. Male and female flowers are yellow and appear on the same plant. A female flower has a short, thick stem and an immature fruit just below the petals. Bush varieties can be grown successfully in large pots, growing bags or other containers. Trailing kinds, grown over trellis or a pergola, will make a novel screen.

CONDITIONS

Aspect Marrows prefer to grow in full sun to partial shade.

Site Thrives in a wide range of soils, but good drainage is essential. Dig in plenty of well-rotted manure and compost several weeks before sowing or planting.

GROWING METHOD

Sowing and planting Raise seeds in pots in gentle heat 4–5 weeks ahead of setting young plants out in the open garden. Sow seeds 1.3cm (0.5in) deep, one per 7.5cm (3in) pot. Alternatively, in late May or June, sow the seeds directly into prepared soil in their final growing position. Set three seeds 2.5cm (1in) deep in a wide saucer-shaped depression of manure-enriched soil that has been fortified with balanced fertiliser. Space seed clusters 60cm (2ft) apart for bush varieties; 120cm (48in) apart for trailing varieties. Thin to the strongest seedling. Keep plants free from weeds and other decaying matter which might harbour disease. Cultivate only lightly, trying not to disturb the delicate root structure. If no fruit develops it may be due to cold weather and/or to a lack of bee activity around the flowers. If this occurs, dust pollen from the male flowers on to the stigma of female flowers to help fruits set.

Feeding Top dress with fish, blood and bone meal when the first fruit has formed and water in at once. Remember, too much fertiliser will promote vigorous growth at the expense of the fruits. Water the root area thoroughly in dry weather, but keep water off stems and foliage. The large leaves may wilt during hot weather, but usually recover if the soil is kept moist.

Problems Powdery mildew, a common disease, is best tackled by applying fungicide. Preventative care is important. Do not handle plants while wet and make sure that air circulates freely between them. Avoid cucumber mosaic virus, which is spread by sucking insects, by growing resistant varieties such as F1 'Tiger Cross'. Aphids can be controlled by spraying with insecticide.

HARVESTING

Picking Marrows mature in 12–14 weeks, depending on variety. Gather fruits when they are 20–25cm (8–10in) long. Finish cropping before the frosts set in. Allow skins to harden before cutting and storing in suspended nets for the winter.

MARROW AT A GLANCE

A frost-tender annual with cylindrical or spherical green, yellow, grey, white or striped fruits in summer or winter.

Month	Activity		Recommended Varieties
Jan	/		**Bush:**
Feb	/		'Green Bush'
Mar	/		F1 'Tiger Cross'
Apr	sow		'Long Green Bush 2'
May	sow		
Jun	sow, transplant		**Trailing:**
July	harvest		'Long Green Trailing'
Aug	harvest		
Sept	harvest		
Oct	harvest		
Nov	/		
Dec	/		

MUSHROOM

Agaricus

AN ABUNDANT CROP of mushrooms can be grown in boxes of composted manure and harvested over a six to eight week period.

FEATURES

The mushroom is a fungus, the edible part being a spore-producing head which grows upwards from a body of filaments feeding throughout a bed of compost below.
Young mushrooms have a small, white, rounded head. Additionally, there is the pine mushroom with deep yellow to golden gills, the golden enoki, white oyster shimeji and shiitake forms. There are also many poisonous wild fungi so careful identification is essential. As the mushroom is not a true vegetable it feeds in quite a different way to vegetables.
After planting in the prescribed manner, greyish coloured filaments (hyphae) appear in approximately 1–2 weeks, spreading throughout the compost. They grow together to form a mesh of fibrous roots/stems called mycelium. Pinhead structures, which develop into mature mushrooms, grow from this mycelium.

CONDITIONS

Aspect Prefers the dark but will tolerate some light. Sunlight is not necessary for growth.

Site The home gardener usually grows mushrooms in dark cupboards or in cellars. Good ventilation is required to remove excessive carbon dioxide in the air. Constant, cool to warm temperatures between 16–18°C are recommended.

GROWING METHOD

Sowing and planting Plant all year round. Buy proprietory packs of sterilised mushroom farm compost, already inoculated with mushroom spawn – usually sold in buckets – and follow the instructions. Alternatively, make your own compost and plant mushroom spawn.
Preparing compost: Ideally, use wheat straw from stables. Stack it, water it and turn it at five-day intervals. It's ready when it is crumbly and dark brown and doesn't smell of ammonia.
Spawning: Put 30cm (12in) of compost into boxes or buckets. When the temperature in the middle of the compost has dropped below 24°C add fungus spawn. There are two types, block spawn (manure impregnated with spawn) and grain spawn (cereal grains infused with spawn).
Push golf ball sized pieces of block spawn into compost, or sprinkle grain spawn over the surface and mix it into the top 5cm (2in).
Keep it warm. Fungus will begin to 'run' in 7–14 days.
Cover the compost with a 5cm (2in) layer of equal parts of moist peat and lump chalk. Maintain a temperature of 16–18°C.

Feeding Water regularly. Do not fertilise. Within about four weeks the mushrooms will be ready for picking.

Problems If mushroom fly maggots tunnel into caps, control them with a permethrin insecticide.

HARVESTING

Picking Button mushrooms are cropped before the cap opens. Mature mushrooms are ripe when the cap opens and the gills are exposed. Twist stalks from the compost and pick regularly to encourage further flushes. If the stalks break off, cut them cleanly and fill holes with covering material. When, after 6–8 weeks, the bed is exhausted, start again with new compost.

MUSHROOM AT A GLANCE

The easiest way to grow mushrooms is to obtain proprietary packs of specially prepared compost impregnated with spawn.

Month			RECOMMENDED VARIETIES
JAN	plant	harvest	As well as the conventional mushrooms, you may be lucky to find Enokitake (Enoki). There are also Shimeji and Oyster mushrooms which are grown on pieces of log.
FEB	plant	harvest	
MAR	plant	harvest	
APR	plant	harvest	
MAY	plant	harvest	
JUN	plant	harvest	
JULY	plant	harvest	
AUG	plant	harvest	
SEPT	plant	harvest	
OCT	plant	harvest	
NOV	plant	harvest	
DEC	plant	harvest	

Button: Small, immature, unopened version of the cultivated mushroom with firm texture and delicate flavour.

Enokitake (Enoki): Rare long stemmed variety. Don't eat stems and remove mucilage from caps before cooking.

Large flat: Fully mature mushroom with soft, strongly flavoured flesh.

Shimeji: Growing in clusters and similar to the oyster mushroom, it has a firm texture and mild flavour. Look out for it.

Varieties

Whichever 'mushroom' appeals to you,
please check on its edibility.

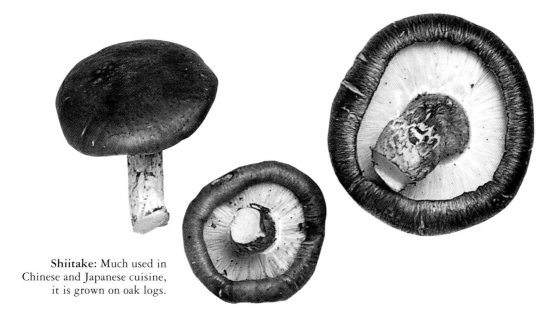

Shiitake: Much used in
Chinese and Japanese cuisine,
it is grown on oak logs.

Swiss brown: Dark-coloured,
immature version of the cultivated
mushroom often served raw,
sliced, in salads.

Oyster mushroom: Clustering on tree
trunks, its pale, fine textured, creamy grey
caps have an oyster flavour.

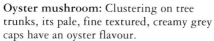

OKRA

Hibiscus esculentus, syn. *Abelmoschus esculentus*

HIBISCUS-LIKE FLOWERS give way to green seed pods which are removed with scissors. Harvest regularly to encourage a long succession.

FEATURES

Also known as gumbo or lady's finger, okra is an annual and a member of the hibiscus family. Large yellow flowers with reddish-purple centres produce edible seed pods which have an unusually high gum content. Because of this, okra is an acquired taste. The green pod is best picked when 5–10cm (2–4in) long. The plant has a long hairy stem and large leaves.

CONDITIONS

Aspect Full sun. Ideally, grow in a greenhouse, in pots or growing bags or outdoors under cloches.

Site Outdoors, okra thrives in clay or loamy soils that are neither over- nor under-fertilised and are cool and moist in summer. The bed may need to be raised if there is any danger of rainwater sitting around the crowns. Mulch thickly to conserve soil moisture. Nitrogen and phosphate requirements are high.

GROWING METHOD

Sowing and planting In late winter or early spring set seeds shallowly, just covering them, in pots of gritty seed compost. Cover the pots with glass and newspaper to shield the soil from light. Germinate in a temperature of 18–21°C. When seedlings appear, set them singly in 7.5cm (3in) pots of multipurpose compost. Grow them on in gentle heat and close to the glass.
In March, in a heated greenhouse, transplant them singly to 25cm (10in) pots, or two to a standard-sized growing bag. When stems are 22.5–30cm (9–12in) high, cut out the growing points to encourage the plant to develop a bushy habit. Stake to stop them flopping.
In early June, when frosts have finished, set the plants 60cm (2ft) apart in cloche-warmed soil. Retain the cloches. The flowers will take from 12 to 14 weeks to appear.

Feeding Greenhouse and outdoors: Liquid feed weekly with a high potash fertiliser when first fruits form, to encourage a long cropping period. Outdoors: Rake in a balanced fertiliser ten days before planting under cloches. As okra is prone to stem rot, water sparingly around but not over the plant.

Problems Guard against stem rot, which is worse in wet conditions, by growing plants in well-drained soil. Rotate crops to avoid a build up of soil diseases. Under glass, ventilate freely when outdoor temperatures are high to ensure a brisk air flow and minimise the risk of pests and disease spores alighting on leaves.

HARVESTING

Picking Gather soft and tender pods when 5–10cm (2–4in) long, from June onwards from greenhouse plants, and September onwards from cloche-grown plants. If left too long, pods become fibrous and tough. Pick daily to lengthen the cropping period.

OKRA AT A GLANCE

Best as a greenhouse crop, okra is grown for its long, green, edible seed pods. It is also called lady's fingers or gumbo.

Month	Activity		Recommended Varieties
Jan	/		'Clemson Spineless'
Feb	sow		'Green Velvet'
Mar	sow		'Long Green'
Apr	transplant		
May	transplant		
Jun	harvest/transplant		
July	harvest		
Aug	harvest		
Sept	harvest		
Oct	/		
Nov	/		
Dec	/		

ONION

Allium cepa

ENJOY TOP RESULTS by growing plants in manured soil and liquid feeding until bulbs begin to swell. Sow Japanese onions for lifting in June, to bridge the gap between the last of the stored bulbs and the first of the spring-sown crop.

FEATURES

This versatile vegetable, raised from seed or sets, can be grown in most soils. The edible part is the fleshy bulb which can be white, yellow or brown through to red. Spring onions are enjoyed for their small white stems and green tops.

CONDITIONS

Aspect Onions need a position in full sun that is cool in early summer. They are very temperature-sensitive. Warm weather and direct sunlight promote bulb development, so exposure to full sun will be necessary at some stage of the growth process. Cool weather promotes top growth. Green, early-maturing spring onions can tolerate partial shade.

Site Onions prefer neutral to slightly limy soil with a pH of not less than 6.5. Prepare beds in autumn by digging in large amounts of any form of well-rotted organic matter.

GROWING METHOD

Sowing and planting Though exhibitors like to sow in gentle heat in January, for transplanting in April and lifting

in July, most gardeners tend to wait until the soil has warmed up in March or early April. Seeds are then sown thinly in drills 1.3cm (0.5in) deep and 22.5cm (9in) apart. Thin seedlings in two stages: first to 5cm (2in) apart, then to 10cm (4in) apart. Additionally, sow Japanese varieties in August to ripen the following June. These are much milder than other varieties. Seeds may also be sown in

ONION AT A GLANCE

A bulbous biennial, grown as an annual, onions can be stored for most of the year. Pull salad onions before bulbs form.

			RECOMMENDED VARIETIES
JAN	sow		**Late summer-autumn:**
FEB	sow		Seed: F1 'Albion'
MAR	sow, plant		'Ailsa Craig Prizewinner'
APR	transplant		Sets: 'Jet Set'
MAY	transplant		'Marshall's Giant Fen Globe'
JUN	harvest		**Early to mid summer:**
JULY	harvest		Seed: 'Imai Early Yellow'
AUG	harvest		Sets: 'Radar'
SEPT	harvest		**Salad onions:** 'Ishikura'
OCT	plant		
NOV	/		
DEC	/		

SPRING OR BUNCHING onions are sown from March to July for pulling from June to October, or in August for a spring crop.

autumn to give you onions that mature slightly earlier than spring-sown bulbs. Salad onions are sown twice a year – in March to May for a June to October crop and from August to early September for a spring harvest. When weeding, try not to cover the maturing bulbs with soil. Bulbs from sets are easier than seed. Sets are planted from mid March to April, for lifting in late summer. They can also be planted in early autumn for lifting from mid June.

Feeding   Give crops a good start by raking in a balanced fertiliser before sowing or planting. Liquid feed while plants are young but stop when bulbs start to swell. If applying a balanced fertiliser, blood, fish and bone meal is best as it builds the soil's vital humus reserves. Water regularly and evenly but ease up when the bulbs start to enlarge, or they may split. Lack of water delays growth and leads to bulb splitting.

Problems   Onion flies attack seed-raised plants in late May, so guard against them by dusting with insecticide containing pirimiphos methyl. If white rot appears, when bulbs develop fluffy, fungal-infested bases, lift and burn plants and do not grow onions on the same patch for at least eight years.

HARVESTING

Picking   When leaves have turned yellow and collapsed, lift bulbs on a dry day. Lay them on a wire frame to dry, covering them if rain threatens. When necks are crisp, store in a dry, airy, frost-free place. Remove loose scales which can hold moisture and cause bulbs to rot. Tie bulbs in ropes or knot them singly in old tights. Pull spring onions when stems are pencil thick.

ONION VARIETIES

From top: 1. Mature brown-skinned onion; 2. White onion; 3: Red onion; 4. and 6. Spring onions; 5. Onion sets.

PARSNIP

Pastinaca sativa

PARSNIPS NEED deeply dug, friable soil to grow well – the roots may fork in hard, stony or freshly manured ground.

FEATURES

A popular and high yielding vegetable, parsnip needs little space and crops over a long period but it is not suitable for container growing. It has a fleshy cream to white tap root which grows to 30cm (12in) or more and from which celery-like leaves appear. The root is rich in sugar, most of which is lost in cooking, but it still has a distinctively sweet taste and aroma which is unusual for a vegetable.

CONDITIONS

Aspect   Full sun to partial shade.

Site   Parsnips need well-drained, organically enriched, deep sandy loam. Prepare soil by digging deeply to allow the tap root to grow straight and true. Ideally, sow parsnip in a bed that has been heavily manured for a previous

crop. Avoid deep hoeing which may damage roots. Mulch to keep roots cool.

GROWING METHOD

Sowing and planting   Sow seeds from late February to April. Seed is not usually viable over long periods so obtain fresh stock each season. Set seeds in clusters of three, 1.3cm (0.5in) deep and 22.5cm (9in) apart, in rows 30cm (12in) apart. Thin the clusters to the strongest seedling when they are 2.5cm (1in) high. Plants will take approximately five months to mature. Hand weed if necessary.

Feeding   Rake in a complete fertiliser a week before sowing seeds or transplanting module-raised seedlings. Do not over-fertilise as too much nitrogen leads to excessive leaf growth and small roots. Water copiously during early stages of growth but ease off as the root thickens. Too much water induces root crack. Too little will lead to slow root development and even to stunting.

Problems   Canker can erode flesh and cause deep brown fissures. Overcome it by growing canker-resisting varieties and by mulching crowns with well-rotted garden compost to stop them from cracking and drying out. Don't incorporate fresh manure as this can cause roots to fork badly. Apply lime if your soil is acid. Don't sow too early – before ground has warmed up – as the seeds may rot. Control leaf-sucking aphids and leaf-blistering celery leaf miner by spraying with insecticide.

HARVESTING

Lifting   Lift roots as required, using a spade to avoid spearing them, from October onwards. They are very hardy. If severe frosts threatens, dig up a batch and box it in sand to draw upon when remaining roots are 'sealed in'.

PARSNIP AT A GLANCE

Harvest the large, fleshy roots of this hardy biennial, treated as an annual, from autumn to late winter.

Month	Activity		Recommended Varieties
Jan	harvest		'Avonresister'
Feb	sow		'Cobham Improved Marrow'
Mar	sow		F1 'Gladiator'
Apr	sow		'Hollow Crown'
May	/		F1 'Javelin'
Jun	/		'Kingship'
July	/		'Tender and True'
Aug	/		'White Gem'
Sept	/		
Oct	harvest		
Nov	harvest		
Dec	harvest		

PEA

Pisum sativum

PICK PEAS WHEN SWEET and tender and before seeds bulge. A succession of sowings yields a wealth of pods from May to September.

THIS CONE-SHAPED OBELISK makes an unusual and decorative support for eat-all and easy to grow sugar snap peas.

FEATURES

Climbing annuals with pretty flowers and green tendrils, there are round- and wrinkle-seeded varieties. The round-seeded varieties are the hardiest and they can be sown in October for cropping the following June. Wrinkle-seeded kinds are always sown in the spring, when the soil has warmed up. Some are grown for the seeds contained in fibrous pods; others for the pods themselves. The garden pea which is grown for its green seeds is the most widely cultivated. Mangetout and sugar snap are both types cultivated for their pods. Sugar snap peas are also sometimes allowed to mature and then shelled and eaten like garden peas. Edible succulent pods of the sugar snap pea resemble the ordinary pea, while the mangetout has flat pods. Small leaflets, tasting just like the pea, are sometimes picked and used in salads. Quick-growing, bushy, dwarf peas can be grown without support; however, they may benefit from propping up with a few twigs to keep pods clear of the ground and slugs and snails. Peas will crop within 3–4 months of sowing.

CONDITIONS

Aspect   Peas prefer to grow in positions of full sun to partial shade.

Site   Beds must be well drained and enriched with organic matter. Acid soils need treating with lime to raise them to a pH level of 6.5. Peas fix nitrogen in the soil through bacterial action in

their root nodules, so after harvesting cut off haulms (stems) and compost them, then dig the stumps into the soil where they will rot down and release nitrogen which will benefit a follow-on crop.

GROWING METHOD

Sowing and planting   Ensure a succession of pods by sowing from February to October or November. Starting in February, set seeds of a round-seeded variety under cloches to produce peas for picking from May to June. Continue with a first early wrinkled kind by sowing in mid March for picking in July. For gathering pods in August, you will need to sow a maincrop variety in April and May. For a fresh pea treat in the autumn, set seeds of a first early wrinkled variety in late June or early July. Mangetout varieties are best sown from March to May, for picking from August to September. A May to June crop is your reward for sowing under cloches in October or early November. Ideally, set the seeds 7.5cm (3in) apart in three staggered rows in a flat drill 15cm (6in) wide and 5cm (2in) deep, taken out with a draw hoe. Firm the soil over the seeds and erect supports when the seedlings are 7.5cm (3in) high. Another method is to use a draw hoe to take out a V-shaped drill, 5cm (2in) deep. Sprinkle seeds thinly in the drill and firm the soil over them. Don't water heavily as this may cause the seeds to rot. Protect seedlings from birds by covering with netting. For tall varieties that need it, and most do, support stems with twigs or netting

THE PRETTY WHITE FLOWERS produced by climbing peas are edible – pick them and use them as a garnish in salads.

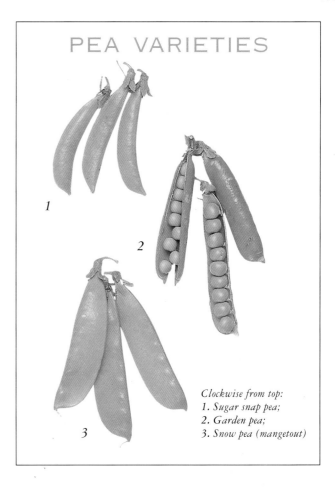

PEA VARIETIES

Clockwise from top:
1. Sugar snap pea;
2. Garden pea;
3. Snow pea (mangetout)

1

2

3

to permit easier cultivation and harvesting. Tall varieties, to 1.2m (4ft) or more, are excellent for summer screens. Position plants where they will hide a compost heap or some other unsightly object. Alternatively, peas can be planted to 'green up' a sunny chainlink boundary fence. Most pods will form on the sunny side.

Feeding Work a complete fertiliser into the soil before sowing the seeds. Use either Growmore or blood, fish and bone meal. Help autumn-sown plants to withstand the winter and crop strongly in the spring by working superphosphate into the root area ten days before sowing. Water peas carefully as they need a cool, moist soil.

PEA AT A GLANCE

Enjoyed for its sweet and tender seeds or succulent pods, the pea is grown as an annual and harvested from spring to autumn.

			RECOMMENDED VARIETIES
JAN	/		
FEB	sow		**First early:**
MAR	sow		'Daybreak'
APR	sow		'Douce Provence'
MAY	sow	harvest	'Feltham First'
JUN	sow	harvest	'Meteor'
JULY	sow	harvest	**Second early/Maincrop:**
AUG		harvest	'Ambassador'
SEPT		harvest	'Cavalier'
OCT	sow		'Hurst Green Shaft'
NOV	sow		'Kelvedon Wonder'
DEC	/		

Problems Practice crop rotation to reduce the incidence of diseases. These can include root rot and pod and leaf rot, which are worse in wet weather. Discolouration of the leaves and pods and the appearance of blackish streaks on the stems also indicate disease.

The worst pest is pea moth, the maggots of which will tunnel into the seeds. Avoid this problem by spraying with insecticide seven to ten days after the flowers open. Mildew, which felts leaves and pods with silvery white mould, is best controlled by spraying with a carbendazim-based fungicide when the disease is first spotted. These sprays should be repeated at fortnightly intervals.

Because peas are prone to several root diseases, do not grow them on the same site for more than one year in three.

Mice can also be a problem as they will devour seeds in chilly weather. If you see mouse droppings, you may have a problem and may need to put down bait and trap these creatures.

HARVESTING

Picking Gather pea pods when they have filled out and are fairly firm and there is still a little air space around the seeds. Use both hands for picking, one to hold the stem, the other to remove the pod. Pick pods regularly to avoid leaving any to grow old as this will check the development of embryo pods. Gather mangetout varieties when they are no more than 7.5cm (3in) long, and the seeds have not yet begun to bulge in the pods.

POTATO
Solanum tuberosum

POTATOES CROP HUGELY ON A SUNNY and liberally manured patch. Lift early varieties when the flowers appear and an exploratory dig reveals tubers the size of a hen's egg. Wait until the leaves die back before lifting maincrop varieties.

FEATURES

Originating in the high mountain regions of South America, frost-tender potatoes have hairy, tomato-like leaves and bear a weighty underground crop of tubers. Depending upon variety, the skin ranges from cream through reddish-brown to dark purple. The flesh is creamy-white to white, and can be floury or waxy. Different varieties lend themselves to a number of cooking techniques. This is an easy vegetable to cultivate and may be grown quite successfully in containers.

CONDITIONS

Aspect Potatoes grow best in full sun.
Site This crop does best when grown in well-drained, fertile soils. The soil must be light and crumbly and high in organic matter, with a pH of 5 to 6. Avoid limy soil as this will increase incidence of scab disease infecting skin, although it will not necessarily affect the flesh of the potato.

GROWING METHOD

Sowing and planting Planting time depends on variety. Initially, chit (sprout) tubers in January or February by placing them in shallow seed trays in a light, cool place indoors. When shoots appear, about six weeks later, plant the tubers outdoors. Use a three-prong cultivator or draw hoe to take out furrows 12.5cm (5in) deep and 60cm (2ft) apart for early varieties, and 75cm (30in) apart for maincrop varieties. Plant earlies 30cm (12in) apart in the rows, and plant maincrop varieties 37.5cm (15in) apart in the rows. When shoots appear, mound soil over them if frost is still a threat. When stems are about 22.5cm (9in) high, earth up rows. Make this easy by forking between rows to loosen soil. The object is to make a flat-topped ridge about 15–20cm (6–8in) high. This will also exclude sunlight from the developing tubers and help to protect them from blight disease, which is the potato's worst enemy. Keep down weeds by shallow cultivation.

Feeding In autumn or winter, dig in liberal amounts of bulky manure. Ten days before planting, rake in a fertiliser high in phosphates to help tubers grow to a good size. Add a further top dressing of high phosphate fertiliser when the haulm (stems) are about 30cm (12in) high. Only maincrop varieties need this second feed. Water regularly to encourage a bounteous crop. Irrigate along the channels which form between earthed up rows. Reduce watering just before harvesting.

Problems Aphids can spread mosaic virus and may need to be controlled with an insecticide. Blight is a fungus that can strike in humid weather in July. When the plant is infected, the leaves and stems are speckled brown and rot. Disease spores quickly infect the tubers, which then also rot. The tuber flesh becomes spotted and finally softens and decomposes. Spraying with mancozeb or a copper-based fungicide at fortnightly intervals in July guards against this disease. Another way to deal with infected plants is to cut off and burn contaminated foliage as soon as any symptoms are seen.

USE A FLAT-TINED FORK to lift crop. Insert it well under the clump and gently raise tubers to the surface. Let them 'sweat' for a few hours before storing them in sacks or boxes in a dry, frost-free shed.

HARVESTING

Lifting   Use a fork to lift early varieties when the flowers are fully open – in June or July – when an exploratory dig reveals that tubers are hen's egg size. Lift maincrop tubers in September or October when the foliage turns brown. Cut it back to near soil level, wait ten days, then fork out the tubers. Leave them to 'sweat' for several hours before storing them in paper sacks or boxes in a dry, airy, frost-free shed. They will keep until early spring.

POTATO AT A GLANCE

A half-hardy perennial, native to South America, its tubers are dug from June to October. Maincrops are stored for winter.

		RECOMMENDED VARIETIES
JAN	/	**First early:**
FEB	chit	'Accent'
MAR	plant	'Concorde'
APR	plant	**Second early:**
MAY	/	'Kestrel'
JUN	harvest	'Marfona'
JULY	harvest	**Maincrop:**
AUG	harvest	'Cara'
SEPT	harvest	'Sante'
OCT	harvest	'Valor'
NOV	/	
DEC	/	

POTATO VARIETIES

There are many varieties of potato in all shapes and sizes. Clockwise from top right: 1. Toolangi delight; 2. Cocktail; 3. Pink eye; 4. Belgian congo; 5. Sebago; 6. Pontiac; 7. New; 8. Bintje; 9. Kipfler

Jackpot: Bell-shaped winter squash with delicately flavoured, pale orange flesh, and creamy yellow to orange skin which softens with cooking.

Delica: 'Delica's 'flattened' dark green and well flavoured fruits swell to around 2.25kg (5lb) and store well.

Gold Nugget: Small and globular with orange skin and flesh, the fruits cluster close to the plant's crown.

Queensland Blue: Worth seeking, its medium-sized round but flattened fruit has deeply furrowed tough grey skin.

PUMPKIN

Cucurbita pepo, C. maxima

FRUITS, which must develop thick, ripe skins before harvesting, mature on trailing stems or bushy growth.

FEATURES

Small- to medium-sized pumpkins belong to the species *C. pepo*. *C. maxima* produces large fruit and is actually a mammoth variety of winter squash grown for 'giant' pumpkin contests. Fruits are borne on long, rambling prostrate stems which can grow to 6m (18ft) or more. There are bush varieties too. Large (10cm (4in) wide), yellow male and female flowers appear on the same plant. Female flowers have short, thick stems showing globular immature fruits. The fruit has a sweet taste, and ranges from yellow to orange-gold in colour. Skins vary from dark green to creamy-yellow, depending on variety. The so-called spaghetti squash is a member of the *C. pepo* pumpkin species.

CONDITIONS

Aspect
Site   Prefers full sun but will tolerate light shade. Good drainage is essential. Pumpkins grow over a long period, so dig in plenty of well-rotted manure and compost several weeks ahead of planting.

GROWING METHOD

Sowing and planting   Raise plants in April by sowing seeds singly, 1.3cm (0.5in) deep, in small pots of seed compost. Germinate them in a heated propagator. Harden off and transplant the seedlings outdoors into prepared soil in early June. Alternatively, in late May or early June dig 30cm (12in) planting holes 1.2m (4ft) apart for trailing varieties and 90cm (3ft) apart

for bush varieties, and fork old manure into the base. Refill with excavated soil, mixing in a balanced fertiliser, such as blood, fish and bone meal. Set seeds in clusters of three, 2.5cm (1in) deep. Thin each cluster to the strongest seedling when true leaves have appeared. Be careful not to disturb the root structure when removing seedlings. Keep the area around the plants free of weeds and other decaying matter which might harbour disease. If no fruit develops it may be because of cold weather or lack of bee activity around the flowers. If necessary, hand pollinate female flowers by removing a ripe male flower, stripping off the petals and dabbing the pollen on to the stigma of a female flower. Nip out tips of trailing varieties when the main shoots are 60cm (2ft) long, to encourage fruiting laterals.

Feeding   Liquid feed weekly with a high potash fertiliser when the first fruit has set. Remember that too much fertiliser will promote vigorous growth of foliage at the expense of fruit development. Water up to but not on the stems and foliage. Large leaves may wilt during hot weather but will normally recover if the soil is kept moist.

Problems   Powdery mildew is common. Preventative care is important. Do not handle plants while wet and practice garden hygiene. Diseases such as mosaic virus are spread by aphids. Remove and burn affected plants. Control aphids, which colonise shoot tips, by spraying with insecticide.

HARVESTING

Picking   Fruits mature within 14–16 weeks of sowing and should be cut before it turns frosty. Gather pumpkins when the stem shrivels to leave a hard, dry stalk and the skin is leathery. Leave a small portion of stem on fruit. Store in a cool, airy frost-free shed, ideally on a slatted shelf.

PUMPKIN AT A GLANCE

Frost-tender bush or trailing annual whose large, spherical, oval or round fruits are cut in autumn for storing in winter.

Month	Activity		RECOMMENDED VARIETIES
JAN	/		'Atlantic Giant'
FEB	/		'Crown Prince'
MAR	/		'Dill's Atlantic Giant'
APR	sow	🌱	'Mammoth Orange'
MAY	sow	🌱	'Munchkin'
JUN	sow, transplant	🌱	'Spellbound'
JULY	/		'Sunny' ('Halloween')
AUG	/		'Triple Treat'
SEPT	harvest	🍂	
OCT	harvest	🍂	
NOV	/		
DEC	/		

RADISH

Raphanus sativus

SOWN IN warm, fertile soil and protected in cold spells, globe-shaped or cylindrical radishes can be harvested for many months of the year.

FEATURES

Summer radishes are a spherical or cylindrical root crop. Long roots grow to 15cm (6in). Smaller, rounded varieties grow to 2.5cm (1in). Both are ideal for containers. They are quick growers with sweet flesh which turns bitter and hot if left in the ground too long. The thin skin ranges in colour from red through to white. This is an easy vegetable to grow. (See page 72 for details of winter radishes.)

CONDITIONS

Aspect Radishes enjoy a moist, sunny or lightly shaded place. In high summer, protect the crop from direct scorching sunlight for a few hours a day. Radishes have a tendency to bolt (go to seed) in hot weather.

Site Rich, deep, sandy loam with high moisture holding capacity is required for rapid growth. Radishes do well where the soil has been manured and fertilised for a previous crop. Mulch beds thickly in hot weather. The ideal pH is 6.5. Add lime to acid soil.

CONDITIONS

Sowing and planting Set seed in prepared soil from February to mid August, for pulling from early spring to late summer. Cloche early sowings to speed growth. Take out seed drills 1.3cm (0.5in) deep and 15cm (6in) apart and cover seeds by tamping soil over them with the back of a rake. If the soil is very dry, take out seed drills 5cm (2in) deep, trickle water from a hose or can along them until the soil is soaked. Return soil to correct depth and sow as before. Ideally, thin seedlings to 2.5cm (1in) apart to encourage roots to swell to a good size. Keep beds free of weeds by regular shallow cultivation. Successive sowings every fortnight or three weeks ensure a continuous crop. Because of the quick-growing nature of radish, it can be planted as an 'intercrop' among slower-growing vegetables such as lettuce, then pulled when the main crop needs extra space.

It can also be used as a marker crop for slow-germinating parsnips. Again, pull roots before parsnips need more room.

Another method is to dig a shallow furrow, sprinkle fertiliser along the bottom, cover with a little soil and then sow seed. Fill in the furrow with fertile top soil and water in. Seedlings take 4–7 days to appear.

Feeding Water thoroughly to keep soil moist during the growing stage. Rake in a complete fertiliser ten days before sowing. Once seedlings are growing well do not add fertiliser as this encourages leaf growth at expense of the developing roots.

Problems Caterpillars of the cabbage white butterfly are pests to watch out for. Early spraying with insecticide based on permethrin or malathion is recommended. Control leaf-puncturing flea beetles by dusting with an insecticide containing pirimiphos-methyl.

HARVESTING

Picking Radishes are ready for pulling within 3–6 weeks from sowing. Pull roots when they are no more than the size of a 10p coin in diameter. Water the soil a few hours beforehand so roots come up cleanly.

RADISH AT A GLANCE

Annual with spherical or cylindrical roots which are pulled at three- to six-weekly intervals from spring until late summer.

			RECOMMENDED VARIETIES
JAN	/		
FEB	sow		'Cherry Belle'
MAR	sow	harvest	'French Breakfast 3'
APR	sow	harvest	'Long White Icicle'
MAY	sow	harvest	'Parat'
JUN	sow	harvest	'Pink Beauty'
JULY	sow	harvest	'Prinz Rotin'
AUG	sow	harvest	'Scarlet Globe'
SEPT	harvest		'Sparkler 3'
OCT	harvest		
NOV	/		
DEC	/		

RHUBARB

Rheum x cultorum

ENJOY AN EARLY CROP by forcing plants in situ *or lifting clumps and speeding them into growth in a dark, warm place indoors.*

FEATURES

Forming a large clump of long chunky pink or greenish stems topped with huge, thin leaves, rhubarb is a hardy perennial that dies back to crown buds in winter. Originally grown as a purgative, it was the French who, in 1778, first discovered it was enjoyable in tarts and pies. Though the stems are edible and harvested from spring to early summer, the leaves are highly charged with oxalic acid which makes them very poisonous. Sticks can be forced into early, succulent growth either *in situ* or in a warm, dark place such as a greenhouse or airing cupboard.

CONDITIONS

Aspect
Rhubarb prefers a sheltered sunny site, where its sticks grow long and fat, but it also tolerates light shade, although the stems will be thinner and leaves larger. A position in full sun also yields sweeter growth.

Site
Rhubarb thrives on all kinds of soil, from heavy clay to sandy loam and peat, but it won't tolerate waterlogging. It also needs feeding heavily. If the soil is poor, enrich it by digging in 11.34kg per sq m (25lb per sq yd) of bulky organic manure or garden compost you've converted into crumbly black humus. If the soil drains badly, set crowns on 15cm (6in) ridges.

GROWING METHOD

Sowing and planting
Prepare planting stations 90cm (3ft) apart each way from October or November to April. Fork in 112g per square metre (4oz per square yard) of Growmore before planting. Set crown buds just below the soil surface and firm them in. Water freely if the soil is dry and frost is not imminent. Plants can be divided when they are established and more than three years old. Lift clumps and use a sharp spade to split them into well budded and rooted sections. Replant them immediately.

Feeding
Keep the root area moist in dry spells and liquid feed with a high nitrogen fertiliser, fortnightly from spring to late summer. In autumn, when leaves have turned brown and withered, sprinkle 56g per sq m (2oz per sq yd) of bonemeal around the crown and hoe it carefully into the surface.

Problems
Stem and bulb eelworm distorts leaves and crown rot kills sticks and buds. There is no remedy for either trouble and affected plants should be dug up and burnt. Set new crowns on a fresh site.

HARVESTING

Picking
Pull sticks from March to July, but do not gather any in the first year after planting, while the plant is becoming established. You can take a few stems from each plant in the second season. Thereafter, gather what you require, but always leave 3 or 4 sticks per plant to help build a bountiful crown for next year.

Forcing
Enjoy an early out-of-season crop by forcing plants *in situ*. From January to February, cover an established crown with a lidded barrel and insulate it with a thick layer of manure. Within five to six weeks, you'll be pulling sweet, pink stalks. Alternatively, and quicker, lift an established clump in winter, leave it on the surface to be frosted for ten days, then plant it in a box of soil and cover it with black plastic to exclude light. Placed in an airing cupboard or greenhouse or a shed heated to around 10–13°C, juicy sticks will be ready for adding to custard within four or five weeks.

RHUBARB AT A GLANCE

Perennial and productive for many years, rhubarb yields juicy sticks from winter to spring.

		RECOMMENDED VARIETIES
JAN	force	
FEB	force	'Cawood Delight'
MAR	plant / harvest	'Glaskin's Perpetual'
APR	harvest	'Hawke's Champagne'
MAY	harvest	'Prince Albert'
JUN	harvest	'Reed's Early Supreme'
JULY	harvest	'Stockbridge Arrow'
AUG	/	'Stockbridge Harbinger'
SEPT	/	'Timperley Early'
OCT	plant	'Victoria'
NOV	plant	
DEC	/	

SALSIFY & SCORZONERA

Tragopogon porrifolius   *Scorzonera hispanica*

RESEMBLING A THIN PARSNIP, *but superior in flavour, salsify is dug as required from autumn to spring. Young shoots can be blanched.*

CULTIVATED LIKE SALSIFY, *black-skinned scorzonera has a milder flavour and edible yellow flowers.*

FEATURES

Salsify is a hardy biennial prized for its white skinned and fishy or oyster-flavoured roots in winter and edible mauve flower buds and flowering stems. Scorzonera, similar in appearance to salsify, but with yellow flowers and broader leaves, has black-skinned and less strongly flavoured roots. Savour young blanched shoots (chards) of both vegetables in spring salads. They are grouped because they are grown in similar ways.

CONDITIONS

Aspect   An open position in full sun, shielded from north and east winds.

Site   Encourage long straight roots by growing plants on relatively stone-free soil that was manured for a previous crop; fresh manure may cause roots to fork. Dig deeply to loosen subsoil, to allow roots to penetrate freely. After gently firming the area, by shuffling slowly over it, rake in 56g per sq m (2oz per sq yd) of balanced fertiliser, such as Growmore.

GROWING METHOD

Sowing and planting   In April or May, take out seed drills 1.3cm (0.5in) deep and 30cm (12in) apart. Set clusters of two or three seeds 15cm (6in) apart in the drill. Firm soil over them with the back of a rake. When seedlings are 2.5cm (1in) high, thin them to the strongest per station. Weed carefully, ideally by hand, as careless hoeing can cut roots and cause them to bleed and die.

Feeding   Water freely throughout spring and summer to ensure robust, unchecked growth and long, fleshy roots. If the soil is sandy and dries quickly, conserve moisture by mulching thickly with rotted garden compost, straw or manure. Alternatively, lay plastic mulching strips between rows. If growth is slow, speed it by liquid feeding weekly with a high phosphate fertiliser from spring to late summer.

Problems   Few troubles beset these plants, but white blister fungus, which causes leaves to develop white blotches, like splashed paint, can be a problem. Control it by spraying with Bordeaux Mixture and destroying badly affected plants.

HARVESTING

Lifting   Use a fork to lift the roots (they are brittle, so don't try and pull them up) from mid autumn to mid spring. Flower buds and flowering shoots, cooked like asparagus, are gathered in summer. Enjoy tender blanched shoots (chards) by cutting back old leaves to 2.5cm (1in) from the base in autumn and mounding 15cm (6in) of soil over them. In spring, when new shoots emerge, unearth them and harvest them.

SALSIFY & SCORZONERA AT A GLANCE

These are fully hardy plants enjoyed for their tender roots in winter and blanched shoots in spring.

JAN harvest	**RECOMMENDED VARIETIES**
FEB harvest	
MAR harvest	**Salsify:**
APR sow	'Giant'
MAY /	'Mammoth'
JUN /	'Sandwich Island'
JULY harvest	**Scorzonera:**
AUG harvest	'Black'
SEPT harvest	'Duplex'
OCT harvest	'Habil'
NOV harvest	'Lange Jan'
DEC harvest	'Russian Giant

SEAKALE
Crambe maritima

IN AUTUMN or winter force seakale into growth in a warm dark place and gather blanched shoots when 12.5–17.5cm (5–7in)long.

FEATURES

In nature, this handsome perennial with large, blue-green leaves and heads of white blossom colonises Northern European sandy and shingle beaches. Very hardy, its stems are blanched and cooked like asparagus. Though plants can be raised from seed sown in spring, it's preferable to grow them from thongs (root cuttings) as the time to harvesting is quicker – two years compared with three.

CONDITIONS

Aspect   Hardy and tolerating low temperatures, it's best grown in an open sunny position.

Site   Enrich soil, which can be slightly acid to slightly alkaline, with bulky organic manure or well-rotted garden compost in autumn or winter. Seakale prefers free-draining sandy soil to heavy clay, and roots deeply so happily tolerates drought conditions.

GROWING METHOD

Sowing and planting   In mid March, rake in a balanced fertiliser, such as fish, blood and bone meal, and plant thongs (selected roots) ten days later. Rub off all but the strongest, central, bud and, using a dibber, set roots 37.5cm (15in) apart in rows 45cm (18in) distant. Cover the crown bud with 5cm (2in) of soil. Keep plants weed free and moist in dry weather. Cut out flowering stems. Plants tend to deteriorate after about seven years so it is best to replace a few each season. In late autumn, lift clumps that are about three years old and remove pencil-thick side roots. Trim them to 7.5–15cm (3–6in) long. Tie in bundles, store in boxes of sand in a cool, frost-free shed for transplanting outdoors in March.

Feeding   Not normally necessary. If growth is slow, speed it by dosing plants weekly with a balanced liquid fertiliser from spring to late summer. In April, invigorate crowns by raking in a balanced fertiliser and mulching with crumbly manure or well-rotted garden compost.

Problems   Control leaf-puncturing flea beetle by dusting with insecticide. Avoid club root, which causes roots to become grossly distorted and die, by liming acid soil, ensuring good drainage and observing a three-year rotation of crops.

BLANCHING

Outdoor forcing   In autumn, two years after planting, when crowns are established, tidy the plants by removing dead and dying leaves. In mid winter, cover plants with lidded seakale forcing pots, or 22.5cm (9in) plastic pots with the drainage holes blocked. Cover containers with a thick layer of straw.

Indoor forcing   Alternatively, from November onwards, shoots can be blanched more quickly in a dark place, in a temperature of 16–21°C. Lift crowns from late September to late October and shorten main roots to 15cm (6in). Remove side roots and plant three main roots to a 22.5cm (9in) pot of rich loamy soil, such as John Innes potting compost No. 3. Water in and cover with an identical sized pot with its drainage holes blocked. Tender young shoots will be ready for cutting within five to six weeks.

HARVESTING

Picking   Gather blanched shoots when 12.5–17.5cm (5–7in) long.

SEAKALE AT A GLANCE

An acquired flavour, new shoots are blanched from late autumn to early spring. Cook them as you would asparagus.

			RECOMMENDED VARIETIES
JAN	force		'Lily White'
FEB	force		
MAR	plant	harvest	
APR	plant	harvest	
MAY	/		
JUN	/		
JULY	/		
AUG	/		
SEPT	/		
OCT	force		
NOV	force		
DEC	force	harvest	

SHALLOT

Allium ascalonicum, A. cepa

HARVESTED from mid to late summer, shallots store well and are easy to grow from sets planted in late winter or early spring.

FEATURES

Shallot bulbs resemble fat garlic cloves in shape and measure 1–3 cm (0.375–1.25in) in diameter when mature. They have a similar flavour to onions, but are milder. Elongated varieties have a stronger flavour than the rounded varieties. Belonging to the *Aggregatum* group, bulbs are clustered at the base of the plant which has slender, tubular green stems. Shallot are used a great deal in French cooking, particularly for making sauces, where their subtle flavour is an asset. This is an easy vegetable to grow.

CONDITIONS

Aspect Shallots prefer to be grown in full sun to partial shade.

Site Dig in large quantities of manure or compost several weeks before planting sets from January to April. Shallow, fibrous roots require light cultivation and beds need to be kept free of weeds.

GROWING METHOD

Sowing and planting After raking a balanced fertiliser into prepared and crumbled soil, take out shallow drills 22.5cm (9in) apart and plant sets 10cm (4in) apart. Just cover them with soil so the dried stem tips are not showing and birds won't then think they are worms and pull them out.
If root pressure forces a bulb to the surface, replant it with a trowel, for to press it back into the soil will damage its roots.
Shallots may also be raised from seed. Less likely to bolt than sets, they are sown from February to late April for cropping in late August. Take out drills 22.5cm (9in) apart and 1.3cm (0.5in) deep and sow thinly. Thin out seedlings, using thinnings in salads, until plants are 10cm (4in) apart.

Feeding Boost growth by liquid feeding with a high potash fertiliser at weekly intervals from spring until the bulbs start to swell. Water regularly.

Problems Beat onion fly, whose larvae tunnel into roots and kill them, by dusting alongside rows with insecticide based on pirimiphos-methyl.

HARVESTING

Picking Bulbs mature in 3–4 months, but can be harvested after 8 weeks if soft bulbs with white stalks and young green leaves are preferred. Young succulent leaves may be used in salads or as a flavouring in the same way that chives are used. Mature bulbs are lifted when leaves wither. Tease soil away from bulb clusters to help them ripen. Finally, when leaves are quite brown, lift plants carefully, split them into single bulbs and dry them on a wire frame in full sun. When the leafy necks are crisp and dry, remove loose scales, which can hold moisture, and store bulbs in netting sacks in a cool, airy, frost-free place for drawing upon in winter.

SHALLOT AT A GLANCE

Shallots have a milder flavour than onions. Delicious pickled, they also add piquancy to winter soups, stews and casseroles.

Month	Activity		Recommended Varieties
JAN	plant		**Sets:**
FEB	plant, sow		'Atlantic'
MAR	plant, sow		'Delicato'
APR	plant, sow		'Golden Gourmet'
MAY	/		'Hative de Niort'
JUN	/		
JULY	harvest		**Seed:**
AUG	harvest		'Atlas'
SEPT	/		F1 'Creation'
OCT	/		F1 'Matador'
NOV	/		
DEC	/		

SPINACH

Spinacea oleracea

SOWN FROM MARCH TO JUNE and again in August for overwintering, spinach can be picked most of the year. Gather leaves frequently to encourage a rapid succession of new ones.

ENGLISH SPINACH likes cool, damp weather and will run to seed in the heat.

FEATURES

Mature spinach produces a rosette of edible dark green leaves 20–27.5cm (8–10in) long with a prominent midrib. Leaves are crinkled or smooth, depending on variety. New Zealand spinach is not a true spinach and produces much smaller leaves than the standard variety. It crops well in hot, dry conditions.

CONDITIONS

Aspect
Site
Sun to partial shade and shelter from wind. Well-drained, rich soils. Thrives in neutral to limy soil enriched with well-rotted manure. Dig in manure in autumn or winter. Lime applied at 112g per sq m (4oz per sq yd) will help to raise pH of acid soils. Keep weeds down by mulching, which also keeps roots cool.

GROWING METHOD

Sowing and planting
Sow summer varieties every three weeks from mid March to late May for picking from June to late October. Set seeds of winter varieties in August and again in September, for harvesting from October to April.
Sow New Zealand spinach when frosts finish in late May, for picking from July to September. For summer and winter varieties take out drills 2.5cm (1in) deep and 30cm (12in) apart and sow thinly. Thin out seedlings first to 7.5cm (3in) apart then remove alternate plants, using thinnings for cooking. New Zealand spinach needs more room. Sow clusters of three seeds 1.8cm (0.75in) deep, 60cm (2ft) apart each way. Thin clusters to the strongest seedling. Lightly

cover seeds with compost and water in so that soil is just moist. Seedlings emerge within 2–3 weeks.

Feeding
A week before planting, rake in a complete fertiliser. When seedlings appear, weekly feeding with a high nitrogen fertiliser will speed rapid and succulent growth. Soil should be moist, but avoid continually wetting leaves.

Problems
Spinach blight will cause leaves to yellow, curl up and die. Remove and burn plants, as there is no cure. Downy mildew, which causes pale patches on leaves, can be controlled by spraying with mancozeb.

HARVESTING

Picking
Crops take 8–10 weeks to mature. Pick individual leaves as required or pull the whole plant from the ground.

SPINACH AT A GLANCE

Spinach produces edible, dark green leaves which can be harvested for most of the year. It needs deep, moisture-retentive soil.

			RECOMMENDED VARIETIES
JAN	harvest		
FEB	harvest		**Summer:**
MAR	sow	harvest	'Dominant'
APR	sow	harvest	F1 'Fordane'
MAY	sow		F1 'Rico'
JUN	harvest		'Sigmaleaf'
JULY	harvest		F1 'Splendour'
AUG	sow	harvest	New Zealand (not true
SEPT	sow	harvest	spinach)
OCT	harvest		
NOV	harvest		**Winter:**
DEC	harvest		'Long Standing'

SQUASH
Cucurbita

CHARACTERISTICALLY FLATTENED and scalloped soft-skinned summer squashes are harvested when about 7.5cm (3in) across

FEATURES

Members of the cucumber family's gourd group, summer squash has a soft skin and is picked and eaten when immature.
Winter squash is left to ripen on the stem and cut when the rind hardens. Fruits are stored for winter and usually keep until Christmas. There are bush and trailing kinds. Create a feature by planting trailing varieties to clamber over an old apple tree, trellis or chainlink fence. When fruits form, net them and tie them to the supporting structure to prevent them breaking the stems.

CONDITIONS

Aspect Full sun to partial shade.
Site Squashes grow in a wide range of soils, but good drainage is essential. They are heavy feeders and need richly fertilised soil, so dig in plenty of well-rotted manure and/or decayed garden compost in autumn or winter.

GROWING METHOD

Sowing and planting Raise seedlings in April, one per small pot, in gentle heat, setting them 1.3cm (0.5in) deep. Harden off for transplanting outdoors in late May or June. Alternatively, sow them outdoors into their final cropping position. If you opt for sowing *in situ,* take out generous planting holes 120cm (4ft) apart for trailing varieties, or 60cm (2ft) apart for bush kinds, and enrich soil with old manure and a sprinkling of

balanced fertiliser. Sow seeds 2.5cm (1in) deep in clusters of three. When the first true leaves form, thin clusters to two plants at the seedling stage and to one healthy plant when true leaves appear. Be careful not to disturb the roots, ideally removing seedlings by cutting stems at ground level. Keep plants free from weeds. Shallow cultivate, trying not to disturb the plant's root structure. If no fruit develops it may be because of cold weather or because of lack of bee activity around the flowers. If this happens, hand-pollinate the female flowers (see pumpkin).

Feeding Encourage robust growth and a good crop by liquid feeding weekly with a high potash fertiliser when first fruit sets. Water freely, but keep the water off the stems and foliage, especially when fruit is setting. Mulch thickly on sandy soils to help conserve moisture. Lack of water may cause partly formed fruit to fall. Large leaves may wilt in hot weather but they usually recover if the soil is moist.

Problems Powdery mildew, whitening leaves, can be remedied with a fungicide. Prevention is important, so do not handle fragile plants while wet, and practise garden hygiene. Aphids spread diseases such as cucumber mosaic virus, so control them with an insecticide. Combat slugs, which will be out in force on warm, damp nights, by sprinkling environmentally friendly blue slug pellets, which the birds have difficulty seeing.

HARVESTING

Picking Summer squashes mature in 12–14 weeks, but are often harvested earlier, before the skin hardens. Gather fruits of winter squashes when the skin becomes leathery but before frosts arrive. Ideally, suspend stored fruits in netting to avoid any pressure on the flesh, which may then rot.

SQUASH AT A GLANCE

Soft-skinned summer varieties and later-maturing kinds for winter storage are easily grown on a sunny, fertilised patch.

		RECOMMENDED VARIETIES
JAN	/	**Summer varieties:**
FEB	/	F1 'Sweet Mama'
MAR	/	'Patty Pan'
APR	sow	'Sunburst'
MAY	sow/transplant	
JUN	sow/transplant	**Winter varieties:**
JULY	harvest	'Autumn Queen'
AUG	harvest	'Butternut'
SEPT	harvest	'Buttercup'
OCT	harvest	F1 'Gemstore'
NOV	/	
DEC	/	

SWEDE

Brassica napus var. *napobrassica*

A TREAT FOR WINTER – delicious in soups and casseroles – roots are dug as required or lifted and stored in boxes of sand in a cool shed.

FEATURES

Swede is also known as 'rutabaga' and is very similar to turnip. It can be identified by multiple leaf scars on top of the root and deeply-lobed, greyish-green leaves. Its large root sits on the soil surface. The skin is white, yellow or purple and the flesh creamy to yellow. It is one of the hardiest crops we have, and often succeeds on dry soil in which turnips are seldom successful.

CONDITIONS

Aspect Thrives in full sun or partial shade.

Site The soil should be well drained, and organically rich to encourage strong root growth. Beds that have been well fertilised and manured for a previous crop are ideal as long as earlier crops were not other brassicas, such as cabbages, Brussels sprouts or broccoli. Try not to let the soil dry out as swedes will not do as well in dry conditions. Keep beds weed-free, hoeing carefully to avoid damaging roots.

GROWING METHOD

Sowing and planting Sow every three weeks, from late April to mid June, for lifting roots from mid September to March. Using a draw hoe, take out drills 1.3cm (0.5in) deep and 37.5cm (15in) apart and sow sparingly. When seedlings are about 2.5cm (1in) high, thin them at intervals to 22.5cm (9in) apart.

Feeding Prepare soil by raking in a high phosphate fertiliser ten days before sowing. When seedlings are growing strongly, augment with weekly applications of a high phosphate liquid feed. Water copiously in periods of hot weather to avoid any check to growth.

Problems Soft rot, which causes leaves to collapse and the crown to decay, is worse in wet seasons. Avoid the problem by growing plants in well-drained soil that does not get waterlogged in winter, by not over-manuring the ground and by practising crop rotation.
Flea beetles may puncture leaves. Guard against them by spraying with insecticide when damage becomes apparent. If club root appears (plants develop grossly swollen and 'fingered' roots), do not sow swedes on the infected site for at least five years, and lime soil liberally. Alternatively, grow 'Marian', a resistant variety.

HARVESTING

Lifting This vegetable reaches maturity in 20–24 weeks. The roots are frost hardy and can be dug as required. Alternatively, it may be more convenient to lift and store them. If you lift them, twist off the leaves from the crown and pack the roots in boxes of damp sand. Store the boxes of roots in a cool place. Alternatively, clamp the roots. Choose a free-draining patch in a sheltered part of the garden and spread a 20cm (8in) thick layer of straw. Build a pyramid of roots on the straw and cover this with more straw to a depth of 20cm (8in). Cover the straw with a 15cm (6in) layer of soil. When you draw upon the roots, cover the remainder carefully to insulate them from severe frosts.

SWEDE AT A GLANCE

Swedes produce large, tasty roots. They are very hardy and can be dug as required, or lifted and stored in boxes of sand.

Month	Activity		RECOMMENDED VARIETIES
JAN	harvest		
FEB	harvest		'Best of All'
MAR	harvest		'Lizzy'
APR	sow		'Marian'
MAY	sow		'Melfort'
JUN	sow		'Ruby'
JULY	/		
AUG	/		
SEPT	harvest		
OCT	harvest		
NOV	harvest		
DEC	harvest		

SWEET CORN

Zea mays var. *saccharata*

PLANT SWEET CORN in a block to ensure that pollen, dispersed by wind from spiky male flowers, alights on and pollinates the female 'silks' (flowers), so that kernels will develop.

THE COB'S silky female flowers darken when kernels ripen.

FEATURES

A member of the grass family, sweet corn grows from 1.2–1.8m (4–6ft) high, producing 1–2 cobs per stem. A cob comprises regularly arranged seeds, called kernels, which are white to yellow, although some varieties have red and black seeds or a combination of all these colours. Corn is pollinated by the fall of pollen from male flowers (tassels) at the top of the stem on to female flowers (silks) lower down.

CONDITIONS

Aspect
Site

Needs full sun and shelter from strong winds. Beds should be heavily fertilised, and watered when growth is vigorous.

SWEET CORN AT A GLANCE

Yielding one or two plump and sugar-rich cobs per stem, wind-pollinated sweet corn is best grown in a block rather than rows.

		RECOMMENDED VARIETIES
JAN	/	
FEB	/	F1 'Conquest'
MAR	/	F1 'Champ'
APR	sow	F1 'Earlivee'
MAY	sow	F1 'Festival'
JUN	transplant	F1 'Incredible'
JULY	/	F1 'Sundance'
AUG	harvest	
SEPT	harvest	
OCT	harvest	
NOV	/	
DEC	/	

GROWING METHOD

Sowing and planting

Grow plants in blocks so that most of the pollen falling from the tassels alights on the silks and fertilises the female flowers.
In the South, sow outdoors in mid May. Take out seed drills 2.5cm (1in) deep and 45cm (18in) apart and set pairs of seed 45cm (18in) apart. Remove the weaker seedling from each pair when plants are 7.5cm (3in) high.
In colder areas, plants should be raised in gentle heat, in a greenhouse in late April, or sow seeds outdoors under cloches in mid May. If sowing under glass, set two seeds 2.5cm (1in) deep per peat pot and thin seedlings to the strongest. Peat pots are best as both plant and pot can be transplanted to avoid any check to growth. Remove cloches when shoots touch the glass or plastic. Mound soil over roots that form at the base of the stem.

Feeding

Dig in manure in autumn or winter. Help pollinated cobs mature quickly by liquid feeding weekly with a high potash fertiliser in spring and summer. Keep soil moist.

Problems

Fruit fly bores into seedlings and causes stunted shoots. Control with insecticide. Birds are liable to nip seedlings. Guard against them by covering rows with tensioned black cotton or netting.

HARVESTING

Picking

Cobs are mature within 12–14 weeks from planting. Check for ripeness by inserting your thumbnail into a kernel. If thin white 'milk' oozes out from the kernel then the cob is ready for harvesting.

SWISS CHARD

Beta vulgaris var. *cicla*

SWISS CHARD, also known as seakale beet or silver chard, yields a large crop of fleshy leaves. Enjoy them lightly boiled with melted cheese.

FEATURES

Swiss chard is a member of the beetroot family and is often mistakenly called spinach. It has white to cream ribbed stems and large, green, crinkly leaves and is cooked and eaten like spinach. All parts of the plant are edible. Rhubarb chard has red stems and Rainbow chard yields plants with red, purple, yellow or white stalks. All are easy to grow and are often interplanted with flowers. This crop grows quickly and is ready for picking within 8–12 weeks of sowing. It may bolt to seed in hot weather.

CONDITIONS

Aspect Thrives in full sun or partial shade.
Site Likes a fertile, free-draining soil. Prepare beds with plenty of compost or decayed manure dug in, in autumn, adding lime to increase the pH if the soil is acid.

GROWING METHOD

Sowing and planting Either sow seeds *in situ* in the garden or in a seed bed and transplant seedlings to their cropping quarters. Two sowings a year – in April and July – ensure almost year round continuity. Prepare soil by raking in a balanced fertiliser. Take out seed drills 2.5cm (1in) deep and 45cm (18in) apart and set seeds sparingly. Cover the seeds and water them in. In dry spells, take out seed drills to twice the recommended depth, trickle water along them until they are saturated, then replace the soil and sow at the usual depth. Seedlings should appear within 2 weeks. Thin them progressively to 30cm (12in) apart (thinnings can be cooked and eaten). Surplus seedlings can be transplanted. They seldom bolt if watered freely when the soil is dry. If flower stems appear, remove them. Keep beds free from weeds and mulch in hot weather.

Feeding Encourage rapid succulent growth by top dressing rows with a balanced fertiliser at monthly intervals from spring to late summer. Keep soil moist by regular watering.

Problems On warm humid nights, slugs can be a menace. Tackle them with blue slug pellets, which birds have difficulty seeing, or watering the soil with a liquid slug killer based on metaldehyde. Guard against leaf-chewing pigeons in winter by covering rows with netting suspended on a wooden frame.

HARVESTING

Picking Swiss chard crops over a long period. Pick mature outside leaves – a few from each plant in turn – when they are 20–37.5cm (8–15in) long. Break them off with a downwards and sideways action. Alternatively, the whole plant can be cropped by cutting it back to 5cm (2in) from the ground and leaving it to regenerate. In autumn, when nights turn chilly, cover the rows with plastic tunnel cloches to keep the plants growing strongly for cutting over the winter.

SWISS CHARD AT A GLANCE		
Large, leafy spinach-like plant with quilted leaves borne on thick, fleshy stalks. Two sowings yield an almost continuous supply.		
JAN	/	**RECOMMENDED VARIETIES**
FEB	/	
MAR	harvest	'Fordhook Giant'
APR	sow	'Ruby Chard'
MAY	/	'White Silver'
JUN	harvest	
JULY	sow harvest	
AUG	harvest	
SEPT	harvest	
OCT	harvest	
NOV	harvest	
DEC	harvest	

TOMATO

Lycopersicon esculentum

'SUNGOLD', a heavy cropping variety for outdoors or the greenhouse, produces long trusses of bite-size deep orange fruit.

BE VIGILANT when cultivating tomatoes: maturing plants need constant protection from disease and marauding pests.

FEATURES

Heavy-yielding tomatoes for greenhouse or outdoors are excellent for growing bags and other containers. Small-fruited varieties are ideal for patio pots and hanging baskets.

CONDITIONS

Aspect   Although preferring full sun, greenhouse tomatoes under glass may be damaged by sun scald. Outdoor plants need protection from strong winds.

Site   Fertile, well-drained soil.

GROWING METHOD

Sowing and planting   **Heated greenhouse:** If you can ensure a minimum temperature of 10–13°C, sow seeds in January for planting out in late February for cropping in early summer.
Unheated greenhouse: Set seed in March for crops from July to October.
Outdoors: Raise plants in late March, harden off, transplant to a prepared site in early June.
Sowing (under glass and outdoors): Set seeds thinly 6mm (0.25in) deep in small pots of gritty seed compost and germinate in gentle heat in a propagator. When true leaves appear, prick out seedlings singly in 7.5cm (3in) pots of multipurpose compost.
Greenhouse culture: When plants are 15cm (6in) high, transplant them singly in 22.5cm (9in) pots of multipurpose compost or three to a standard growing bag. Tie stems to vertical canes fixed to overhead wires. Mist flowers daily to help fruits set. Nip out side shoots. Cut out growing point two leaves above topmost truss of fruit when plants have reached full height – normally seven trusses high. Water freely to keep compost evenly moist and

TOMATO AT A GLANCE

Prized for red, yellow or striped orange/red fruits, there are greenhouse and outdoor varieties for harvesting from May to October.

JAN	sow	**RECOMMENDED VARIETIES**	
FEB	sow	**Greenhouse:**	
MAR	sow	'Buffalo'	
APR	transplant	'Golden Cherry'	
MAY	transplant	'Gourmet'	
JUN	harvest	F1 'Shirley'	
JULY	harvest	'Sweet 100'	
AUG	harvest	'Yellow Pear'	
SEPT	harvest	**Outdoor (cordon):**	
OCT	harvest	'Ailsa Craig'	
NOV	/	'Gardener's Delight'	
DEC	/	**Outdoor (bush):**	
		'Roma VF'	

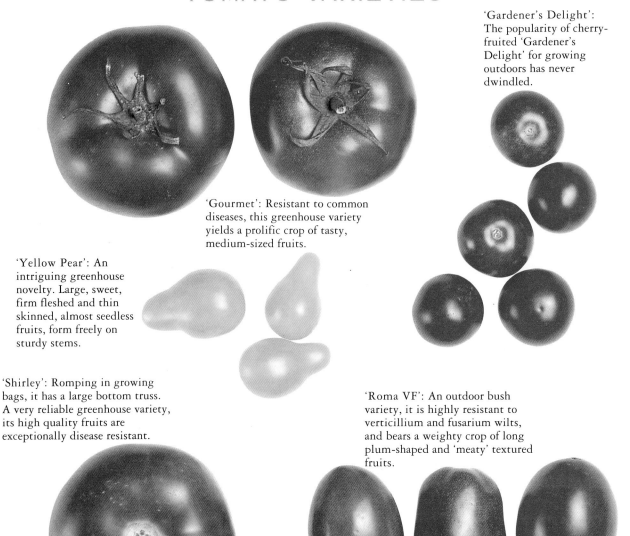

'Gardener's Delight':
The popularity of cherry-
fruited 'Gardener's
Delight' for growing
outdoors has never
dwindled.

'Gourmet': Resistant to common
diseases, this greenhouse variety
yields a prolific crop of tasty,
medium-sized fruits.

'Yellow Pear': An
intriguing greenhouse
novelty. Large, sweet,
firm fleshed and thin
skinned, almost seedless
fruits, form freely on
sturdy stems.

'Shirley': Romping in growing
bags, it has a large bottom truss.
A very reliable greenhouse variety,
its high quality fruits are
exceptionally disease resistant.

'Roma VF': An outdoor bush
variety, it is highly resistant to
verticillium and fusarium wilts,
and bears a weighty crop of long
plum-shaped and 'meaty' textured
fruits.

liquid feed as described below. When sun heat
strengthens, shade glass with blinds or paint.
Outdoor culture: When frosts are no longer a
risk, set plants in soil manured in autumn or
winter. Enrich site with a balanced fertiliser
raked in ten days before transplanting. Set
cordon varieties 38–45cm (15–18in) apart each
way and bush varieties 45–60cm (18–24in)
apart. Small bush varieties are planted
25–30cm (10–12in) apart. Before planting
cordons, insert 1.5m (5ft) supporting canes and
tie plants to them. Remove sideshoots when
5cm (2in) long. Water freely in dry spells.

Feeding   Liquid feed weekly with a high potash
fertiliser when the first fruits swell.

Problems   Greenhouse varieties: Tackle whitefly by
spraying every three days for at least a month,
with a permethrin-based insecticide, and
suspending sticky cards above the crop. Beat

tomato leaf mould by spraying with
carbendazim. Avoid blossom end rot by keeping
compost moist at all times.
Outdoor varieties: Avoid blight, which causes
leaves to become brown, speckled and die and
fruit to rot, by spraying with a mancozeb
fungicide at fortnightly intervals from early July.

HARVESTING

Picking   Gather fruits when fully coloured, by breaking
them off at the knuckle, to leave a small stalk.
Outdoor varieties: Help green fruits ripen by
removing canes from cordon plants and laying
plants on a bed of straw. Cover with cloches.
Alternatively, pick fruits and ripen them in a
drawer with a couple of ripe apples. The
ethylene gas from apples speeds the process.

TURNIP

Brassica campestris rapa

SOWN FROM MARCH TO SEPTEMBER, early varieties taste best when golf ball sized. Lift and store maincrop roots in October.

FEATURES

A vegetable related to swede. The turnip's large swollen root has white flesh and skin topped by a rosette of feathery leaves. Both leaves and root are edible, though turnip is mainly grown for its root which is sliced raw in salads, or used to flavour soups and stews. Leafy tops of young plants can be boiled like spinach. Early varieties can be flattish or spherical and are usually white. Main crops are normally spherical, and white, yellow or white with a green top.

CONDITIONS

Aspect   Prefers full sun, but summer sowings tolerate light shade.

Site   Beds should be deeply dug and crumbled before sowing to encourage roots to make penetrating growth. Ideally, choose an area that was well manured for a previous crop and not, within the previous year, planted with any other brassica, such as cabbage.

GROWING METHOD

Sowing and planting   Enjoy a tasty succession of roots by sowing periodically from late winter to September. Set seeds of early varieties under cloches in February or March, or set the seeds outdoors from late March to April for crops that can be harvested from May to September.
Raise maincrop varieties for storing from October onwards, by sowing the seeds outdoors from mid July to mid August.
Fancy spring greens? Sow a maincrop variety from August to September. Prepare soil by raking in a balanced fertiliser ten days before taking out seed drills 1.3cm (0.5in) deep. Space rows 22.5cm (9in) apart for early varieties, 30cm (12in) for maincrop kinds, and 7.5cm (3in) for turnip tops (spring greens). Sow thinly. When seedlings are 2.5cm (1in) high, thin them at intervals to 12.5cm (5in) apart for earlies or 22.5cm (9in) apart for maincrop varieties. Hoe carefully to behead weeds.

Feeding   Spur growth, if slow, by liquid feeding with a high phosphate fertiliser at weekly intervals in spring and summer. Water freely during dry spells.

Problems   Leaf-puncturing flea beetles can be a pest in dry weather. Check them by dusting with a permethrin-based insecticide. Soft rot, a condition which starts with collapsing foliage and a slimy, rotten crown, is worse in wet seasons. Defeat it by growing plants on well-drained soil and hoeing carefully to avoid damaging seedlings. Practise a three-year crop rotation.

HARVESTING

Lifting   Roots are ready for pulling within 6–12 weeks. Gather early varieties when golf ball sized if you wish to slice them into raw salads. Leave them to swell to midway between golf ball and cricket ball size if you intend to cook them. Lift maincrop varieties in early autumn for storing over winter in a cool, airy but frost-free place. Dig up roots with a fork and twist off leaves 2.5cm (1in) from the crown. Pack in boxes of damp sand.

TURNIP AT A GLANCE

Succulent roots which can be stored for winter use are your reward for sowing from spring to late summer.

		RECOMMENDED VARIETIES
JAN	/	
FEB	sow	**Early:**
MAR	sow harvest	'Gold Ball'
APR	sow harvest	'Market Express'
MAY	sow	'Purple Top Milan'
JUN	sow harvest	'Snowball'
JULY	sow harvest	F1 'Tokyo Cross'
AUG	sow harvest	
SEPT	sow harvest	**Maincrop:**
OCT	harvest	'Green Globe' (also for
NOV	harvest	spring greens)
DEC	harvest	

WINTER RADISH

Raphanus sativus var. longipinnatus and var. radicola

MILD-FLAVOURED 'Mino Early' prospers in organically rich soil. Its roots can be 5cm (2in) across and more than 30cm (12in) long.

FEATURES

Unlike summer varieties (see page 59), winter radishes are hardier and produce huge roots. White Japanese 'mooli' types can grow to 5cm (2in) across and 20cm (8in) long.
Chinese and Spanish varieties are usually globular, with red, black, violet or white skin, and they can develop roots that weigh in at 450g (1lb) or more.
They are normally peeled before cooking or pickling. The flavour is stronger than that of a summer radish. The flesh is white to greenish in colour. Plants grow to 30–60cm (1–2ft). A non-branching stem supports a leafy rosette.

CONDITIONS

Aspect Though it prefers full sun, it will tolerate light shade.
Site Soil should be organically rich and well manured for a previous crop. Avoid digging in fresh manure as this may cause the roots to fork. Don't sow on heavy clay soil which doesn't allow seedlings to penetrate easily.

GROWING METHOD

Sowing and planting Fork soil deeply and rake in a balanced fertiliser ten days before sowing in July or early August. Using a draw hoe, take out seed drills 1.3cm (0.5in) deep and 22.5cm (9in) apart. Sow the seeds thinly, about 2.5cm (1in) apart. Thin the seedlings progressively until they are about 15cm (6in) apart. Large-rooting varieties will need up to 22.5cm (9in) of space around each plant. As the seedlings grow, their swelling roots should be covered with soil.

Feeding Do not feed the plants after raking in the initial balanced feed, for extra food given late in the year will encourage frost-tender growth. Water steadily and constantly and do not let the soil dry out. As plants reach maturity, reduce the amount of watering as excess water will lead to cracking of the roots of winter radishes.

Problems Control aphids and cabbage white caterpillars with pyrethrum sprays. Avoid bacterial soft rot, which affects roots at ground level, gradually making them soft and mushy, by practising crop rotation.
Handle this crop carefully during cultivation and destroy diseased plants. Thwart flea beetles, which make pepperpot holes in leaves, by spraying with insecticide containing permethrin. Slugs may also be a menace in mild spells. Control them by scattering blue slug pellets, or by watering the soil with a liquid molluscicide.

HARVESTING

Lifting Winter radishes will mature within 8–10 weeks, but they can be harvested at any stage. They are ready for harvesting when about 20cm (8in) long (for elongated varieties) or when their diameter is 5–10cm (2–4in). Skins should be smooth and flesh firm. Use a spade to lift roots from late October onwards. If a sharp frost is forecast, store roots in boxes of damp sand, in a cool airy, frost-free place, after twisting off the leaves 2.5cm (1in) from the crown.

WINTER RADISH AT A GLANCE

Sow in summer for an autumn harvest of weighty roots up to 30cm (12in) long. Flavour is stronger than summer varieties.

Month		RECOMMENDED VARIETIES
JAN	/	'Black Spanish Round'
FEB	/	F1 'Cherokee'
MAR	/	'China Rose'
APR	/	'Mantanghong'
MAY	/	'Mino Early'
JUN	/	
JULY	sow	
AUG	sow	
SEPT	sow	
OCT	harvest	
NOV	harvest	
DEC	harvest	

WITLOOF
Cichorium intybus

ENJOY a winter and early spring feast of tender, cigar-shaped chicons by forcing roots into growth in a warm, dark place.

FEATURES

Also known as Belgian chicory, witloof is prized for its blanched, lettuce-like heart (chicon). When forced into growth in a warm, dark place, the shoot resembles a plane's nose cone. Its whitish yellow leaves have a bitter-sweet taste. Enjoy chicons cooked or raw. To cook, boil in salted water and allow to simmer for 15–20 minutes. After draining, cover with cheese sauce. Alternatively, braise them for 20 minutes in butter. If you haven't tried them before and want to eat them raw in salads, add tomatoes to temper their bitter-sweet flavour.

CONDITIONS

Aspect   Grows best in bright sunlight.
Site   Not fussy about soil, but it must be organically well endowed, so dig in manure in autumn and winter.

GROWING METHOD

Sowing and planting   Prepare soil by raking in a balanced fertiliser ten days before sowing seeds in May and June. Take out seed drills 1.3cm (0.5in) deep and 30cm (12in) apart and set seeds thinly. When seedlings are 2.5cm (1in) high, thin youngsters to 15cm (6in) apart. Water freely and keep down weeds. If the soil is thin and sandy, conserve moisture by mulching thickly with well-rotted garden compost or old manure. Alternatively, lay perforated black plastic between rows. In November, lift parsnip-like roots and cut off leaves 2.5cm (1in) above the crown. Retain the fattest roots – not less than 2.5cm (1in) across – and shorten them to 15cm (6in). Pack them horizontally in boxes of damp sand and store them in a cool, dark and airy place.

Feeding   If extra food is necessary to stimulate growth, top dress rows with fish, blood and bone meal, but do not apply this later than August. Witloof needs regular watering to keep the soil moist, especially through the hotter months.

Problems   Control slugs with pellets or liquid molluscicide. Guard against cutworms, which sever leaves at soil level, by applying an insecticide based on pirimiphos-methyl.

HARVESTING

Blanching   When plants are required for forcing, in a dark place, from November to March, plant five roots upright in a 22.5cm (9in) pot, packing peat or potting compost between them. The crowns should be 2.5cm (1in) above the compost surface. Water in. Cover the pot with another of the same size, with the drainage holes blocked, and position it in a temperature of 10–16°C to encourage chicons to form.

Picking   The crop takes about 4 months to mature from sowing. The second stage of cultivation (blanching) takes about 8–12 weeks. Chicons will then be 15–20cm (6–8in) long and ready for cutting. Use a sharp knife and sever them just above the crown. After harvesting, water lightly and replace cover. With luck, a further batch of smaller chicons will appear.

WITLOOF AT A GLANCE		
Enjoyed for its fleshy, torpedo-shaped, blanched shoots, forced into growth in gentle heat from autumn to spring.		
JAN	force	RECOMMENDED VARIETIES
FEB	force	'Apollo'
MAR	force	F1 'Witloof Zoom'
APR	/	
MAY	sow	
JUN	sow	
JULY	/	
AUG	/	
SEPT	/	
OCT	/	
NOV	force	
DEC	force	

NAME	STORAGE
ASPARAGUS	Fresh asparagus will keep in the refrigerator for 7–10 days after being harvested. Break off the rough ends and stand upright in 2.5cm (1in) water.
AUBERGINE	Fruit will keep for 7–10 days in a cool spot. It is ideal for pickling.
BEAN, RUNNER	Do not wash after harvest. Freshly picked pods will keep in a refrigerator for up to a week or they can be successfully bottled or pickled when mature.
BEETROOT	Lift roots in autumn, twist off leafy tops, and store the roots sandwiched between damp sand in a box in a cool, frost-free place.
BROAD BEAN	Freshly harvested pods will keep in refrigerator for up to two weeks. Shelled beans can be dried, or preserved by bottling.
BROCCOLI	Heads will keep in refrigerator for up to a week, after which vegetable gradually turns yellow and becomes tasteless.
BRUSSELS SPROUT	Buttons left on the stem and hung in a cool dry place will keep for up to a month. Remove all loose and discoloured leaves from the plant and only wash the sprouts just before you are ready to use them. Singly harvested, they will keep for 7–10 days in a refrigerator.
CABBAGE	After cutting, use spring and summer varieties within ten days. Harvested white winter varieties will keep for weeks if you remove the stem and outer leaves and pack heads in straw-lined boxes in a cool, dry place.
CAPSICUM	Capsicum, or sweet peppers, will keep for up to a week in a refrigerator. They can also be grilled or baked, and with the skins and seeds removed, preserved in spicy vinegars. Hot chillies can be dried successfully.
CARROT	Carrots can be stored *in situ* if the soil is well drained. Cover crowns with straw if hard frost threatens. Leave the leafy tops attached. Once cropped, the top can be removed 2.5cm (1in) above the crown and the roots stored in containers packed with damp sand. Store in a cool, frost-free place. Carrots will also keep crisp in refrigerator for 4 weeks or so if protected in plastic bags. They are delicious pickled or bottled.
CAULIFLOWER	Heads will keep for up to a week in the refrigerator. Florets can be pickled.
CELERIAC	In cold areas and in free-draining soils, 'bulbs' can be left *in situ*. Cover with straw if hard frost is forecast. Alternatively, on heavy soil and in cold areas, lift 'bulbs' in November and cut off leafy tops just above the crown. Store in boxes of sand in a cool, frost-free shed.
CELERY	Celery stalks will keep crisp for up to 10 days in a refrigerator. Leaves can be dried and chopped and used as a dried herb for flavouring purposes. Seeds can also be dried, and used in soups and pickles.
CHILLIES	Keep in a cool, dark place for up to a week or in a sealed container in refrigerator for 3 weeks. Chillies are also excellent when dried.

VEGETABLES

NAME	STORAGE
CHINESE BROCCOLI	Pick shoots at flower bud stage and use as soon as possible. Can be kept for a week or so in a sealed plastic bag in a refrigerator.
CHINESE CABBAGE	Keeps fresh for several weeks in a refrigerator or in a cool, dry place, such as a cellar. When ready to use, discard outer discoloured leaves to reveal firm, central head. Never store in plastic bags.
COURGETTE	Handle carefully and do not wash or brush skin of fruit before use. Fruits will keep for up to a week in refrigerator.
CUCUMBER	Will keep in refrigerator for 7–10 days, but at very cold temperatures the flesh will turn soft and translucent, rendering the cucumber inedible. It is ideal for pickling if the fruit is picked when young, that is, at the 'gherkin' stage, and 5–7.5cm (2–3in) in length.
ENDIVE	Chicons will keep for up to a fortnight in the salad compartment of a refrigerator. The blanched inner leaves are best for salads.
FLORENCE FENNEL	Bulbs cannot be stored and should be eaten as soon as possible after cutting.
FRENCH BEAN	Do not wash pods after harvest. Freshly picked pods will keep in refrigerator for up to a week, or they can be bottled or pickled.
GARLIC	When leaves turn yellow, lift bulbs and dry them in a warm, breezy spot outdoors. When leaves are crisp at the neck of the bulb, plait the bulbs into a rope or hang in bunches.
GLOBE ARTICHOKE	Harvested buds will keep in a cool place for several weeks or in the refrigerator for no more than a fortnight. Keep them dry in an airtight plastic bag.
JERUSALEM ARTICHOKE	As with other root crops, the simplest method of storing is to leave tubers in the ground, digging only when required. Alternatively, lift tubers and keep them for a month or so in boxes of damp sand in a cool, dark, frost-free place.
KALE	Pick and use leaves as required. Leaves will keep for a week or so in the salad compartment of a refrigerator.
KOHL RABI	Pull as required and use immediately, or store in a refrigerator for 7–10 days.
LEEK	Will keep 7–10 days in refrigerator. Alternatively, lift plants and pack in boxes of soil. They will keep for several weeks in a cool, dark place.

Storing

NAME	STORAGE
LETTUCE	Will keep for 7–10 days in the salad compartment of a refrigerator.
MARROW	Handle carefully and do not wash or brush skin of fruit before use, to prevent deterioration. For winter use, wait until the skin is leathery before cutting in early autumn. Suspend fruit in a net in a cool, dark place.
MUSHROOM	Mushrooms can be stored in the refrigerator in paper bags (not in plastic bags or they will sweat) for around 5–7 days. They can also be dried, or pickled and stored in jars.
OKRA	Pods stay crisp for a week or so if packed in a plastic bag and stored in a refrigerator.
ONION	Store ripened bulbs in a cool, dry, airy and frost-free place. Hang them in bunches, rope them, or pack them in old tights or nets. They will keep for months.
PARSNIP	Parsnips can be left in the ground and dug as required. Low temperatures convert starches to sugars giving a sweet root. They will also keep for 2–3 weeks in a refrigerator.
PEA, INCLUDING MANGETOUT AND SUGAR SNAP	Pick as required. Pods keep for a short time in a refrigerator, but within a few days the seeds will lose a great deal of their sugar content, which is converted to starch.
POTATO	Store only maincrop varieties for winter, as earlies do not keep well. After lifting, allow tubers to 'sweat' and dry on the soil surface before packing in paper, hessian sacks or boxes. Keep cool and frost-free, and in a dark place to stop tubers turning green.
PUMPKIN	Handle carefully and do not wash or brush skin of fruit before storing. Fruit will keep for several months in a cool, airy place. Sit fruit on slatted shelves, or net and suspend them. Check occasionally for rotting.
RADISH (SUMMER)	Roots will keep for 7–10 days in the salad compartment of a refrigerator.
RHUBARB	Cook as soon as possible after pulling. Stalks will stay plump for a few days in a cold place.
SALSIFY AND SCORZONERA	Dig as required, or lift and cut off leaves just above the crown and pack the roots into boxes of just-damp sand. Enclose roots in a plastic bag and keep in a refrigerator. They will keep fresh for a week or so.

VEGETABLES

NAME	STORAGE
SEAKALE	Cut the blanched shoots and use them as soon as possible. They will only keep fresh for two or three days in a refrigerator.
SHALLOT	Pack bulbs in netting sacks. (See onion.)
SPINACH	Spinach leaves will keep in refrigerator for up to a week but they are better if eaten straight away.
SQUASH	Handle carefully and do not wash skin of fruit before use to prevent damage. They will keep for up to a week in a refrigerator. Use summer squashes as soon as possible. Store winter squashes as for pumpkins.
SWEDE	Swedes are dug as required or lifted, leaves removed, and packed in boxes of damp sand. Store in a cool shed. They will also keep for a long time in a refrigerator.
SWEET CORN	Sweet corn kernels are rich in sugar which quickly turns to starch. After the cobs are cut they lose a great deal of their flavour. Freshly picked cobs should be eaten as soon as possible, but they will keep tasty in a refrigerator for a couple of days. Alternatively, strip kernels from the cob and freeze them.
SWISS CHARD	Swiss chard will keep for up to 2 weeks in the salad compartment of a refrigerator, but is best eaten when freshly picked, before leaves wilt.
TOMATO	Tomatoes will keep for 2–4 weeks in a refrigerator although they tend to lose their flavour over long periods. Alternatively, pulp and bottle them or process into soups and sauces and freeze.
TURNIP	Early varieties are dug and eaten as required. Only maincrops are stored. Lift roots in October, cut off leaves 2.5cm (1in) above the crown, and pack roots in boxes of damp sand. Keep in a cool place.
WINTER RADISH	Dig as required. Cover rows with straw to insulate roots from frost, and sprinkle pellets to keep slugs away. If the soil is heavy and inclined to waterlogging, lift roots and store in boxes of sand in a cool but frost-free place.
WITLOOF	Witloof chicons do not store well and become limp soon after exposure to light. May be kept in refrigerator for a few days but if they are exposed to light the leaves will become green and bitter.

NAME	TO FREEZE
ASPARAGUS	Wash and remove woody portions and scales of spears, cut into 15cm (6in) lengths and blanch in boiling water for 3 minutes. Cool in iced water for 3 minutes, drain. Place on trays in a single layer and freeze for 30 minutes. Pack into suitable containers, seal and label. Freeze for up to 6 months.
AUBERGINE	Cut into slices, sprinkle with salt and allow to stand for 20 minutes. Drain off excess liquid and fry slices gently in butter or margarine until just tender. Cool, then pack in plastic containers, seal and label. Will freeze for up to 3 months.
BEAN, RUNNER	Remove any strings and top and tail. Blanch for 2 minutes and cool in iced water for 2 minutes. Drain, spread on tray in a single layer and freeze for 30 minutes. Pack into freezer bags, remove air from bags, seal and label. Freeze for up to 6 months.
BEETROOT	Only freeze young tender beetroots, not more than 5cm (2in) across. Cook until tender and slice, chop or leave whole. Cool and transfer to plastic containers, cover with lids and label. Freeze for up to 6 months.
BROAD BEAN	Shell beans and after washing blanch in boiling water for $1^1/2$ minutes. Cool in iced water for 1–2 minutes. Place on tray in a single layer and freeze for 30 minutes. Pack into freezer bags, remove air, seal and label. Freeze for up to 6 months.
BROCCOLI	Choose tender young heads with no open flowers. Wash well and divide into sprigs. Blanch for 3 minutes in boiling water. Cool in iced water for 3 minutes. Drain and spread on tray in a single layer. Cover with plastic wrap to stop the strong smell of broccoli penetrating the freezer, and freeze for 30 minutes. Pack in freezer bags, remove air from bags, seal and label. Freeze for up to 6 months.
BRUSSELS SPROUT	Remove outer leaves and cut a cross at the stem end of sprout. Wash thoroughly and then blanch for 3 minutes. Cool in iced water for 3 minutes, drain and spread on tray in a single layer. Cover with plastic wrap to prevent strong odour of sprouts penetrating the freezer. Freeze for 30 minutes, remove from tray and pack into plastic bags. Remove air from bags, label and seal. Freeze for up to 6 months.
CABBAGE	Remove outer leaves and wash the remainder. Cut into thin wedges or shred. Blanch for $1^1/2$ minutes if shredded, or 2 minutes if cut into wedges. Chill in iced water for 1–2 minutes. Drain and pack in freezer bags, label and seal. Freeze for up to 6 months.
CAPSICUM	Wash, remove seeds and cut into slices or leave whole. Place on a tray in a single layer. Freeze for 30 minutes. Pack in freezer bags, remove air, label and seal. Freeze for up to 6 months.
CARROT	Wash and scrub carrots and cut large roots into pieces. Blanch for 3 minutes in boiling water. Chill in iced water for 3 minutes, drain well. Spread on a tray in a single layer and freeze for 30 minutes. Pack in freezer bags, remove air from bags, label and seal. Freeze for up to 6 months.
CAULIFLOWER	Divide into florets and wash. Blanch for 3 minutes in boiling water. Chill in iced water for 3 minutes. Drain and place on a tray in a single layer. Cover with plastic wrap to prevent strong odour of cauliflower penetrating the freezer. Freeze for 30 minutes. Transfer to freezer bags, remove air from bags, label and seal. Freeze for up to 6 months.
CELERIAC	Remove leaves. Wash and peel roots and cut into small cubes; blanch in boiling water for 3 minutes. Cool in iced water for 3 minutes, drain and pack into freezer bags. Will keep for up to 6 months.

Vegetables

NAME	TO FREEZE
CELERY	Use young tender stalks. Remove any string and wash and cut into 2.5cm (1in) pieces. Blanch for 2 minutes in boiling water. Chill in iced water for 2 minutes. Drain and place on tray in a single layer. Freeze for 30 minutes. Pack in freezer bags, remove air, label and seal. Freeze for up to 6 months.
CHILLIES	Remove seeds, wash, dry and spread on a tray in a single layer. Freeze 30 minutes, pack in freezer bags, remove air, seal and label. Freeze for up to 6 months.
CHINESE BROCCOLI	Remove any coarse leaves and thick stems. Wash and blanch in boiling water for 2 minutes. Chill in iced water for 2 minutes. Drain and spread on a tray in a single layer for 30 minutes. Pack in freezer bags, remove air, seal and label. Freeze for up to 6 months.
CHINESE CABBAGE	Only freeze crisp and young cabbage. Wash and shred finely. Blanch for 1$^{1}/_{2}$ minutes. Chill in iced water for 1–2 minutes. Drain, and place in freezer bags, label and seal. Freeze for up to 6 months.
COURGETTE	Slice into 2.5cm (1in) sections, without peeling, then saute gently in a little melted butter until tender. Cool, then pack into plastic containers, leaving space at the top of the container. Freeze for up to 3 months.
CUCUMBER	Peel and chop in food processor. Pack into plastic containers with well-fitting lids, label and freeze. Freeze for up to 3 months.
ENDIVE	Do not freeze.
FENNEL	Use fresh young stalks. Wash thoroughly. Blanch for 3 minutes. Chill in iced water for 3 minutes. Drain, pack in freezer bags and remove air from bags. Will freeze for up to 6 months.
FRENCH BEAN	Top and tail. Blanch for 2 minutes and cool in iced water for 2 minutes. Drain, spread on tray in a single layer and freeze for 30 minutes. Pack into freezer bags, remove air from bags, seal and label. Freeze for up to 6 months.
GARLIC	Place cloves, separated from bulbs, in freezer bags. Remove any excess air from bag, seal and label. Freeze for up to 3 months.
GLOBE ARTICHOKE	Remove outer leaves. Wash, trim stalks and remove 'chokes' and blanch them, a few at a time, for 7 minutes. Cool in iced water for 7 minutes, then drain. Pack in freezer bags, remove air from bags, seal and label. Freeze for up to 6 months.
JERUSALEM ARTICHOKE	Peel and slice. Place in cold water with the juice of half a lemon to prevent discolouration. Blanch for 2 minutes in boiling water. Cool in iced water for 2 minutes. Drain and spread on tray in a single layer. Freeze for 30 minutes. Pack into freezer bags, remove air, seal and label. Freeze for up to 6 months.
KALE	Wash tender leaves and blanch in boiling water for 1–1$^{1}/_{2}$ minutes. Chill for 1–2 minutes in iced water. Drain and pack in plastic freezer bags. Will keep for around 6 months.
KOHL RABI	Wash well, peel and cut into pieces. Blanch for 3 minutes. Chill in iced water for 3 minutes. Drain and spread on a tray in a single layer. Freeze for 30 minutes. Pack in freezer bags, remove air, seal and label. Freeze for up to 6 months.
LEEK	Remove tough outer leaves, wash remainder. Cut away green part of stem, slice white flesh, or cut in halves lengthwise. Blanch 2 minutes (slices), or 3 minutes (halves); chill in iced water for 2–3 minutes. Freeze on trays in single layer for 30 minutes. Remove, pack in freezer bags, expel air, seal and label. Freeze for up to 6 months.

NAME	TO FREEZE
LETTUCE	Do not freeze.
MARROW	Peel, cut into pieces and cook in boiling water until just cooked. Cool and place in freezer bags, remove air from bags, seal and label. Alternatively, bake in oven until almost cooked. Cool, package in freezer bags, seal and label. Freeze for up to 3 months.
MUSHROOM	Cultivated mushrooms need no preparation. Pack clean mushrooms in freezer bags. Remove air from bags, seal and label. Freeze for up to 6 months.
OKRA	Wash well and trim off stems. Blanch in boiling water for 3–4 minutes. Cool in iced water for 3–4 minutes, drain and pack in freezer bags. Remove air from bags, seal and label. Freeze for up to 6 months.
ONION	Peel, chop or cut into rings. Wrap in layers of plastic wrap, place in a plastic container. Label and freeze for up to 3 months. Alternatively, package small onions in their skins in freezer bags. Remove air from bags, label and seal. Freeze for up to 3 months.
PARSNIP	Peel and dice. Blanch for 2 minutes, chill in iced water for 2 minutes, then spread on a tray and freeze for 30 minutes. Pack into freezer bags, remove air, label and seal. Freeze for up to 6 months.
PEA	Shell, wash, and blanch for 1 minute. Chill in iced water for 1 minute, drain, spread on a tray. Freeze for 30 minutes. Pack into freezer bags, remove air, seal and label. Freeze for up to 6 months.
POTATO	There are a number of ways of freezing potatoes. (a) Scrub new potatoes. Cook in boiling water until almost cooked. Drain, cool, pack in freezer bags. Seal, label and freeze for up to 6 months. (b) Prepare chips and deep fry for about 4 minutes until cooked, but not brown. Drain and cool on paper towels. Place on a tray in a single layer and freeze for 30 minutes. Pack in freezer bags, remove air, label and seal. Freeze for up to 3 months. (c) Potatoes may also be mashed or prepared as Duchesse potatoes and then frozen for up to 3 months.
PUMPKIN	Peel and cook in boiling salted water until tender. Mash, cool, then pack into plastic containers, leaving headspace. Freeze for up to 3 months. Alternatively, peel and cut into pieces. Bake until almost cooked. Pack into freezer bags when cool, remove the air, seal and label. Will freeze for up to 3 months.
RADISH (SUMMER)	Do not freeze.
RHUBARB	Pull young, tender stems and remove leaves. Cut stalks into 2.5cm (1in) chunks and blanch for about 1 minute. Cool in iced water for 1 minute. Drain, dry and sprinkle with sugar before packing in freezer bags. Will keep for about six months.
SALSIFY	Do not freeze.
SCORZONERA	Do not freeze.
SEAKALE	Do not freeze.

VEGETABLES

NAME	TO FREEZE
SHALLOT	Separate cloves from bulb. Place in freezer bags, remove excess air. Freeze for up to 3 months.
SPINACH	Wash well and trim leaves off stalks, blanch in small quantities in boiling water for 1 minute. Chill in iced water for 1 minute, drain, then pack in plastic bags or containers; label and seal. Will freeze for up to 6 months.
SQUASH	Peel and cook in boiling salted water until tender. Mash, cool and pack into freezer containers leaving room at the top for expansion. Seal and label. Freeze for up to 3 months.
SUGAR SNAP PEAS	Remove pods, wash and blanch for 1 minute. Chill, drain and spread on a tray. Freeze for 30 minutes, then pack in plastic bags, remove air from bags, seal and label. Will freeze for up to 6 months.
SWEDE	Only use tender, young swedes. Cut to required size and blanch for 3 minutes. Chill in iced water for 3 minutes. Drain, place pieces on a tray in a single layer and freeze for 30 minutes. Pack in freezer bags, remove air, seal and label. Freeze for up to 6 months.
SWEET CORN	Remove leaves and threads and cut off top of cob. Wash, blanch a few cobs at a time for 5–7 minutes, depending upon size. Chill in iced water for 5–7 minutes, drain, then wrap each cob in plastic wrap. Pack wrapped cobs in freezer bags, remove air from bags, label and seal. Freeze for up to 6 months.
SWISS CHARD	Wash well and trim leaves from stalks. Blanch in small quantities of boiling water for 1 minute. Chill in iced water for 1 minute, drain, then pack in freezer bags or containers. Remove air from plastic bags, label and date bags or other containers and freeze. Will freeze for up to 6 months.
TOMATO	There are various ways of freezing tomatoes. (a) Wash, remove stems, cut into halves or quarters or leave whole. Dry and pack into freezer bags. Remove air, label and seal. Freeze for up to 6 months. (b) Dip into boiling water for 1 minute, remove and peel. Place whole tomatoes on a tray and freeze for 30 minutes. Place in plastic bags, remove air, seal and label. Freeze for up to 6 months. (c) Simmer chopped tomatoes in a pan for 5 minutes or until soft. Push through a sieve or food mill to remove skins and seeds. Cool, then pack in plastic containers, leaving space at the top of container. Will freeze for 6 months.
TURNIP	Peel and trim young, tender turnips. Cut to required size and blanch for 3 minutes, chill in iced water for 3 minutes. Drain, place pieces on a tray in a single layer and freeze for 30 minutes. Pack into plastic bags, remove air, seal and label. Freeze for up to 6 months.
WINTER RADISH	Do not freeze.
WITLOOF	Wash well. Blanch for 3 minutes. Drain, place on a tray in a single layer and freeze for 30 minutes. Pack into plastic bags, remove air, seal and label, or pack in containers leaving some space at top. Freeze for 2–3 months.

PLANT COMMON NAME	SPRING	SUMMER	AUTUMN	WINTER
Asparagus	●	●		
Aubergine		●		
Bean, runner		●	●	
Beetroot	●	●	●	
Broad bean	●	●		
Broccoli	●		●	●
Brussels sprout	●		●	●
Cabbage	●	●	●	●
Capsicum		●	●	
Carrot		●	●	●
Cauliflower	●	●	●	
Celeriac			●	●
Celery		●	●	●
Chillies		●	●	
Chinese broccoli		●	●	●
Chinese cabbage		●	●	●
Courgette		●	●	
Cucumber		●	●	
Endive		●	●	
Florence fennel		●	●	
French bean		●	●	
Garlic		●		
Globe artichoke		●		
Jerusalem artichoke	●		●	●
Kale	●		●	●
Kohl rabi		●	●	

PLANT COMMON NAME	SPRING	SUMMER	AUTUMN	WINTER
Leek	●		●	●
Lettuce	●	●	●	●
Marrow		●	●	
Mushroom	●	●	●	●
Okra		●	●	
Onion	●	●	●	
Parsnip	●		●	●
Pea	●	●	●	
Potato		●	●	
Pumpkin			●	
Radish (summer)	●	●	●	●
Rhubarb	●	●		●
Salsify			●	●
Scorzonera			●	●
Seakale	●		●	●
Shallot		●		
Spinach	●	●	●	●
Squash		●	●	
Swede	●		●	●
Sweet corn		●	●	
Swiss chard	●	●	●	●
Tomato		●	●	
Turnip	●	●	●	●
Winter radish			●	●
Witloof	●			●

HARVEST RECIPES

Everyone who grows their own vegetables knows that after the excitement of the first few meals using home-grown produce, boredom can set in. A chorus of "not parsnips again!" from the family is enough to break a gardener's heart. Fortunately there are lots of ways to use a glut of vegetables. These recipes allow you to preserve vegetables – some for just a few days, some for several months – which means you can enjoy the produce of your garden long after harvesting.

FRIED ARTICHOKES WITH GARLIC AND CHILLI

7 medium artichokes

juice of 2 large lemons

2 tablespoons plain flour

2–3 tablespoons olive oil

salt, to taste

3–4 whole garlic cloves, peeled

2 tablespoons capers, drained

2–3 chillies, finely chopped

450ml (¾ pint) virgin olive oil

1. Remove all hard outer leaves from artichokes until only a few light green inner leaves and artichoke hearts remain. Using a sharp knife, cut tops from leaves. Brush all cut areas with lemon juice to prevent any discolouration. Dust artichokes in flour; shake off excess.
2. Heat oil in large frying pan; add artichokes and cook until soft. Remove artichokes from pan, drain well on paper towels and sprinkle with salt.
3. Pack artichokes, garlic, capers and chillies into large glass jar. Cover with virgin olive oil. Cool completely, then refrigerate.

NOTE: Artichokes will keep for 4–5 weeks in the refrigerator.

GREEN BEAN RELISH

1kg (2¼lb) green beans

3 onions

1.5litres (2½ pints) malt vinegar

350g (12oz) sugar

1 teaspoon salt

½ teaspoon pepper

1 tablespoon plain flour

1 tablespoon dry mustard

1 teaspoon turmeric

4 tablespoons malt vinegar, extra

1. Top and tail beans and slice diagonally. Peel and thinly slice onions.
2. Combine vinegar, sugar, salt and pepper in large pan. Bring to the boil, stirring, until sugar dissolves. Add the prepared beans and onions; bring to the boil, then reduce heat and simmer, uncovered, until the beans are just tender.
3. Blend flour, mustard and turmeric with extra vinegar. Add to pan and stir over high heat until mixture boils and thickens. Reduce heat and simmer for 5 minutes. Spoon mixture into warm, sterilised jars and seal. Store until required.

BEETROOT ORANGE CHUTNEY

500g (1lb 2oz) beetroot

2 large green apples, peeled and cored

2 oranges

175g (6oz) soft brown sugar

250ml (8fl oz) red wine vinegar

1. Preheat oven to moderate 180°C (350°F, gas mark 4). Brush a baking tray with oil. Trim leafy tops from beetroot and wash thoroughly. Place beetroot on prepared tray and bake for 1 hour 15 minutes or until very tender. Set aside to cool. Peel skins from beetroot and cut flesh into small cubes.
2. Cut apples into small cubes. Peel oranges, removing pith from peel and flesh. Cut the peel into thin strips and chop orange flesh, discarding any pips. Place prepared orange rind and flesh in a large pan; add apple, sugar and vinegar. Stir over medium heat until boiling. Reduce heat and simmer, covered, for 30 minutes.

3. Add the cubed beetroot and simmer for another 15 minutes. Cool slightly and spoon the chutney carefully into warm sterilised jars and seal.

NOTE: Chutney will store for up to 6 months.

PICKLED BEETROOT AND EGG

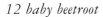

12 baby beetroot

1 bunch dill, chopped

8 hard-boiled eggs, peeled

8 black peppercorns

2 cloves garlic, finely sliced

450ml (³/4 pint) red wine vinegar

4 tablespoons sugar

salt, to taste

1. Trim beetroot, leaving 5cm (2in) stalk intact; leave root whole. Wash thoroughly and place in large pan; cover with water and bring to boil. Reduce heat and simmer, covered, for 1 hour or until beetroot is tender. Remove from pan and cool. Reserve 250ml (8fl oz) cooking liquid.
2. Remove skin from beetroot and break off stalks. (Remove roots if you prefer.) Pack beetroots, dill, eggs, peppercorns and garlic into a large sterilised jar.
3. Combine reserved beetroot liquid, vinegar and sugar in a bowl. Stir until sugar has dissolved; add salt, to taste. Pour mixture over beetroot mixture so that it is completely covered. Seal and refrigerate.

NOTE: Store in refrigerator for up to a week. Serve pickled beetroots with cold sliced ham and a green salad.

PICKLED RED CABBAGE

1 medium red cabbage

75g (3oz) salt

2 tablespoons sugar

pickling spices such as peppercorns,
    juniper berries or allspice berries

300ml (¹/2 pint) cider vinegar

1. Cut cabbage into quarters and discard the tough central core. Shred cabbage finely. Place in a large non-metal dish; add salt and mix through the cabbage. Place a weighted plate on cabbage and leave for 24 hours to draw excess moisture.
2. Rinse cabbage thoroughly and drain on paper towels. Pack tightly into a large, warm, sterilised jar, layering with sugar and spices.

Cover with vinegar and seal. Leave for 2–3 weeks before serving.

NOTE: Pickled cabbage will keep for up to 6 months but should be refrigerated once opened. This is a 'quick' version of the classic German sauerkraut – a fermented cabbage pickle that is traditionally made in wooden barrels which takes approximately 1 month to prepare.

GARLIC PEPPERS

2 green peppers

2 red peppers

4 cloves garlic, peeled and thinly sliced

100g (4oz) sugar

1 litre (1³/4 pints) white vinegar

1 tablespoon salt

1. Cut peppers lengthways into quarters. Remove seeds and membrane. Place peppers in a large pan of boiling water for 1 minute. Remove from pan and cool. Place peppers and garlic in large sterilised glass jar.
2. Combine sugar, vinegar and salt in pan; stir over medium heat until sugar and salt have dissolved.
3. Pour hot liquid over peppers; seal and store for at least 1 week before opening.

NOTE: Garlic peppers store well for up to 6 months. Serve with other antipasti.

RED PEPPER SOUP

2 large red peppers

1 tablespoon oil

1 large onion, chopped

2 cloves garlic, chopped

1 teaspoon grated ginger

2 x 425g (15oz) cans tomatoes, crushed

1.25 litres (2¹/4 pints) chicken stock

soured cream, to serve

1. Cut peppers into pieces, removing seeds and membrane, and flatten out. Place under a hot grill and cook until skins are black (about 5 minutes). Remove from heat and cover with a damp tea-towel. Allow to cool, then peel off skins and discard.
2. Heat oil in a pan. Add chopped onion, garlic and ginger; cook over medium heat for 5 minutes. Add peppers, tomatoes and stock, bring to the boil and simmer for 20 minutes. Allow to cool.
3. Process soup in blender until smooth. Reheat before serving with a swirl of soured cream, if desired.

CARROT AND RHUBARB PRESERVE

1kg (2¼lb) carrots, peeled and thinly sliced

1kg (2¼lb) rhubarb, thinly sliced

1kg (2¼lb) sugar

1. Cook carrots in a large pan of boiling water 10 minutes or until tender. Drain, reserving 250ml (8fl oz) cooking liquid.
2. Process carrots and reserved liquid in food processor until smooth. Transfer to large pan; add rhubarb and sugar.
3. Stir mixture over medium heat until sugar has dissolved. Bring to the boil, reduce heat and simmer, uncovered, 20 minutes or until thickened. Spoon cooled mixture into warm, sterilised jars and seal.

NOTE: Will store for up to 1 month in the refrigerator. Use preserve as a filling for sponge cakes or fruit tarts.

PICKLED CAULIFLOWER

100g (4oz) salt

1.25 litres (2¼pints) water

1 large cauliflower

1.2 litres (2 pints) cider vinegar

2 tablespoons sugar

1 teaspoon whole cloves

1 teaspoon whole allspice

1 teaspoon peppercorns

2 cinnamon sticks

5 dried red chillies

6 radishes

1. Combine salt and water in large pan and stir over low heat until salt is dissolved. Chop cauliflower coarsely. Place cauliflower in large bowl and cover with the salted water. Cover with dry cloth and stand overnight. Drain.
2. Place vinegar, sugar, cloves, allspice, peppercorns, cinnamon and chillies into a pan. Bring slowly to boil and simmer, covered, for 15 minutes. Strain and retain liquid and spices separately.
3. Chop radishes and combine with drained cauliflower. Pack into warm, sterilised jars and add whole cloves, allspice, peppercorns, cinnamon and chillies. Return vinegar to heat and bring to the boil. Pour boiling liquid over vegetables and seal. When cool, label and date.

NOTE: Store in a cool, dark place for 2 weeks before use. This will enhance the flavour of the cauliflower.

GREEN CURRY PASTE

2 tablespoons oil

2 large onions, finely chopped

2 tablespoons ground coriander

20 large green chillies

2 tablespoons grated fresh ginger

8 cloves garlic, peeled

5cm (2in) piece lemon grass

½ teaspoon fish sauce

5 tablespoons lemon juice

½ teaspoon caster sugar

salt, to taste

4 tablespoons oil, extra

1. Heat the oil in a large frying pan; add onions and cook 3 minutes or until softened. Add coriander and cook for 1 minute.
2. Cut the chillies in half lengthways and remove seeds and membrane. Chop finely and place in food processor; add onion mixture, ginger, garlic, lemon grass and fish sauce. Process for thirty seconds or until almost smooth.
3. Add lemon juice, sugar and salt and process briefly. With motor constantly running, add oil in a slow stream until well combined. Spoon into warm, sterilised jar and seal.

NOTE: Paste will keep in refrigerator for up to 10 days.

CHILLI OIL

600ml (1 pint) vegetable oil

3 fresh whole chillies

1 cinnamon stick

2 teaspoons black peppercorns

fresh, whole pieces of chosen flavourings – herbs or whole spices

1. Heat the oil in a large heavy-based pan. Add the chillies, cinnamon stick and peppercorns. Remove from heat, then cover and leave to stand for 2–3 days.
2. Strain the oil into a sterilised bottle. Add fresh, whole flavourings of your choice to the bottle.
3. Seal and label. Store the chilli oil in a cool, dark place.

NOTE: Fresh herbs such as rosemary, basil, sage or lemon grass may be substituted for the chillies.

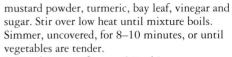

MIXED VEGETABLE PICKLE

450g (1lb) cucumbers, peeled and diced

450g (1lb) onions, chopped

450g (1lb) green tomatoes, chopped

450g (1lb) green beans, chopped

450g (1lb) celery, finely chopped

450g (1lb) small cauliflower florets

450g (1lb) hard white cabbage, shredded

4 tablespoons cooking salt

1.2 litres (2 pints) malt vinegar

225g (8oz) sugar

5 tablespoons dry mustard

3 tablespoons plain flour

1 tablespoon turmeric

1. In a large bowl, combine all vegetables. Sprinkle with salt. Cover with cold water and let stand for 24 hours. Drain. Add half the vinegar and let stand for 12 hours.
2. In small bowl, mix sugar, mustard, flour, turmeric and a small amount of remaining vinegar. In saucepan, bring remaining vinegar to a boil. Stir in mustard mixture. Reduce heat. Simmer 2 minutes. Add vegetables and liquid. Bring to boil and simmer for 20 minutes, stirring often.
3. Pack hot pickle into clean, hot jars. Wipe rims of jars with clean, damp cloth. Cover. Let mature one month before using.

MUSTARD PICKLE

3 medium cucumbers, chopped

1 large onion, chopped

1 large green pepper, chopped

200g (7oz) cauliflower, in tiny florets

2 tablespoons salt

2 teaspoons brown mustard seeds

2 tablespoons mustard powder

1/2 teaspoon turmeric powder

1 bay leaf

250ml (8fl oz) malt vinegar

50g (2oz) sugar

1 tablespoon cornflour

1. Combine cucumbers, onion, pepper and cauliflower in a large non-metal bowl. Sprinkle with salt, leave to stand overnight.
2. Wash and drain the vegetables, rinsing thoroughly to remove all salt. Place in a large heavy-based pan. Add the mustard seeds,

mustard powder, turmeric, bay leaf, vinegar and sugar. Stir over low heat until mixture boils. Simmer, uncovered, for 8–10 minutes, or until vegetables are tender.
3. Combine cornflour and 2 tablespoons water in a small mixing bowl. Add to pan and stir through the vegetables quickly. Bring to the boil, then remove from heat once the mixture has thickened.
4. Spoon into hot, sterilised jars and seal immediately. Label and date when cool.

OLD-FASHIONED BREAD AND BUTTER CUCUMBERS

1kg (2 1/4lb) cucumbers, washed and thinly sliced

2 large white onions, cut in thin wedges

2 tablespoons salt

1.25kg (2 1/2lb) sugar

350ml (12fl oz) white wine vinegar

1 tablespoon mustard seeds

1 teaspoon turmeric

1/4 teaspoon cayenne pepper

1. Combine cucumbers, onion wedges and salt in a bowl. Add enough water to completely cover. Let stand for 2 hours. Drain thoroughly on paper towels.
2. Place sugar, vinegar, mustard seeds, turmeric and cayenne pepper in a large heavy-based pan. Cook, stirring, over medium heat until sugar has dissolved. Add cucumber and onion mixture. Cover, reduce heat and cook gently for 10 minutes, stirring occasionally, until cucumber becomes transparent. Remove from heat.
3. Cool for 15 minutes. Spoon into sterilised jars and seal. Allow to stand for 1 week before using.

AUBERGINE RELISH

2 large aubergines

100ml (4fl oz)oil

4 cloves garlic, crushed

2 green peppers, chopped

2 onions, finely chopped

15g (1/2oz) fresh basil, chopped

1. Chop aubergines into small cubes. Heat oil in large pan; add aubergine, garlic, peppers and onion. Cook, stirring, 5 minutes or until softened.
2. Remove from heat; add basil and stir through. Cool mixture; spoon into airtight container and refrigerate.

NOTE: Aubergine Relish will store for up to a week in the refrigerator. Serve with curries or add to sandwiches.

AUBERGINE AND WALNUT PASTE

2 large aubergines

3 tablespoons olive oil

1/2 teaspoon finely chopped chilli

*3 green peppers, seeded, halved and
    finely chopped*

2 garlic cloves, finely chopped

100g (4oz) walnuts

2 teaspoons sherry

2 tablespoons olive oil, extra

1/2 teaspoon salt

virgin olive oil

1. Preheat oven to moderate 180°C (350°F, gas mark 4). Cut aubergines in half lengthways, sprinkle aubergine flesh with salt and allow to stand 10–15 minutes. Rinse well and drain on paper towels. Place aubergines, cut-side up, on a baking tray. Bake 20 minutes or until flesh is soft; cool. Scoop out flesh and place in food processor.
2. Heat oil in frying pan; add chilli, peppers and garlic and stir over medium heat until vegetables are soft. Transfer to food processor; add walnuts, sherry, extra olive oil and salt.
3. Process mixture 1–2 minutes or until smooth. Spoon the paste into warm, sterilised jars. Top with a thin layer of virgin olive oil and seal.

NOTE: Keeps 3–4 weeks in the refrigerator.

GARLIC VINEGAR

16 cloves garlic

salt, to taste

1 litre (1 3/4 pints) white wine vinegar

1. Peel garlic and crush lightly with a little salt. Place in a large, sterilised, glass container; add vinegar.
2. Seal container and shake well. Store in a cool, dark place 2–3 weeks, shaking the container from time to time.
3. Pour vinegar through muslin-lined funnel into sterilised bottles. Can be used at once.

NOTE: Store vinegar for up to 8 months.

ROASTED GARLIC PASTE

10 whole heads garlic

100ml (4fl oz) oil

salt and pepper, to taste

olive oil, extra

1. Preheat oven to moderate 180°C (350°F, gas mark 4). Using a sharp knife, cut tops off garlic. Pour olive oil over exposed flesh; season with salt and pepper.
2. Wrap 2 or 3 heads at a time in foil and place in baking dish. Roast 1–1 1/2 hours or until flesh is very soft; cool.
3. Squeeze garlic flesh into sterilised jar; drizzle with a little extra oil to just cover.

NOTE: Garlic paste will keep for 2–3 months in the refrigerator. Use paste in sauces, salad dressings, and pasta dishes. Garlic has a much milder flavour once cooked, so do not be alarmed by the quantity of garlic in this recipe.

LEMON GINGER BUTTER

2 lemons

250g (9oz) butter

3 tablespoons grated fresh ginger

2 cloves garlic, crushed

1. Remove peel from lemons and grate finely.
2. Beat butter until light and creamy; add ginger, garlic and lemon peel. Beat until smooth.
3. Using cling film, form into a log shape and refrigerate.

NOTE: Lemon ginger butter can be stored 2 weeks in refrigerator or frozen for up to 3 months. Slice off rounds as they are needed, and return to freezer.

PICKLED GINGER

225g (8oz) fresh ginger

sea salt

250ml (8fl oz) rice wine vinegar

3 tablespoons sugar

red food colouring

1. Peel ginger and cut into thin slivers. Place in a mixing bowl and cover with cold water. Leave to stand for 30 minutes. Drain ginger; place in a pan of boiling water. Bring back to boil, drain and cool in mixing bowl; sprinkle with salt.
2. Combine vinegar and sugar in small pan. Stir over low heat until sugar has dissolved. Add a few drops of red colouring and stir.
3. Pour vinegar and sugar mixture over ginger. Cover with cling film and let stand in a cool, dark place for 2–3 weeks before serving.
4. Place the ginger and pickling liquid into a warm sterilised jar. Seal and label.

NOTE: Store pickled ginger in the refrigerator. Serve with Japanese dishes such as sushi or with chicken or seafood.

JERUSALEM ARTICHOKE RELISH

2kg (4½lb) Jerusalem artichokes

4 onions

2 green or red peppers

1 teaspoon dill

1 teaspoon mustard seeds

1 teaspoon turmeric

1 litre (1¾ pints) cider vinegar

500g (1lb 2oz) sugar

1. Peel artichokes and chop finely. Chop onions. Remove seeds and membrane from peppers and chop finely. (Vegetables can be processed briefly in food processor, but should retain a coarse texture.)
2. Place in a large pan; add dill, seeds, turmeric, vinegar and sugar. Stir over low heat until sugar has dissolved. Bring to the boil, reduce heat and simmer, uncovered, for 30 minutes or until vegetables are tender.
3. Cool slightly and spoon into warm, sterilised jars; seal.

NOTE: Relish will keep several months but should be refrigerated once opened. Serve with a cheese platter or with roasted meats.

DRIED LEEKS AND ARTICHOKES

juice of 2 medium lemons

8 medium artichokes

1 large lemon

8 leeks

1. Preheat oven to very low, 120°C (240–250°F, gas mark ½). Pour about 1 litre (1¾ pints) water into a bowl and add lemon juice.
2. Using a sharp knife, remove and discard outer leaves of 1 artichoke until only inner leaves and heart are left. Cut lemon in half and rub over artichoke to prevent discolouration. Trim green tops from inner leaves, cut artichoke in half and remove choke using a teaspoon. Rub again with lemon, then put in bowl of water and lemon juice while preparing remaining artichokes in same way.
3. Remove artichokes from water, cut into quarters and rub again with lemon.
4. Discard roots and green leaves from leeks, leaving only white stems. Halve leeks lengthwise, then cut into 2.5cm (1in) slices. Wash thoroughly and drain on paper towel. Arrange leeks on a wire grill and place on oven rack with artichokes.
5. Leave in oven for about 4 hours, or overnight, until artichokes and leeks are completely dry. Allow to cool, break into pieces using fingers, mix together and store

in airtight boxes for up to a year.

NOTE: Artichokes will naturally turn dark as they dry, even after rubbing with lemon. Use these dried vegetables in risottos or pasta sauces by soaking 1½ cupfuls of dried artichokes and leeks in 450ml (¾ pint) of warm water for about 4 hours before cooking.

CONFIT OF ROASTED LEEKS

2kg (4½lb) young leeks

100ml (4fl oz) olive oil

2 teaspoons salt

2 teaspoons sugar

1. Preheat oven to moderate 180°C (350°F, gas mark 4). Clean leeks thoroughly, discarding roots and leaves. Cut into 0.5cm (¼in) slices.
2. Layer leeks 2cm (¾in) deep in a well-greased shallow baking tray. Drizzle with olive oil and sprinkle with salt and sugar.
3. Roast, turning often, for 45 minutes to 1 hour, or until leeks appear caramelised and creamy gold.
4. Allow to cool then spoon into dry, sterilized jars; seal.

NOTE: Store roasted leeks in refrigerator for up to 2 weeks. Serve warm or cold in sandwiches, as a pizza topping or to enrich soups or stews.

PICKLED MUSHROOMS

675g (1½lb) mushrooms

1 tablespoon grated fresh ginger

rind of 1 lemon

1 onion, thinly sliced

l litre (1¾ pints) white wine vinegar

salt and pepper, to taste

1. Wipe mushrooms with a damp cloth and trim the stalks to level with the cap.
2. Combine mushrooms, ginger, lemon rind, onion, vinegar, salt and pepper in large pan. Bring to the boil, reduce heat and simmer 20 minutes or until tender.
3. Remove mushrooms with a slotted spoon and transfer to warm, sterilised jars. Strain cooking liquid and return to the boil. Pour liquid over mushrooms, covering them well. Seal and refrigerate.

NOTE: Pickled mushrooms will not keep as long as many other types of pickled vegetables. It is best to use them within 2 weeks of bottling.

GUMBO

500g (1lb 2oz) okra

425g (15oz) can whole tomatoes

50g (2oz) butter

1 large onion, finely chopped

1 green pepper, finely chopped

2 short celery stalks, finely sliced

2 cloves garlic, chopped

2 teaspoons tomato paste

2 teaspoons white pepper

2 teaspoons ground black pepper

1 1/2 teaspoons cayenne pepper

2 teaspoons dried thyme

1/2 teaspoon dried oregano

2 bay leaves

1/4 teaspoon ground allspice

2 teaspoons chilli flakes

1 tablespoon Worcestershire sauce

250ml (8fl oz) chicken stock

1. Combine okra and (undrained) tomatoes in a pan. Bring to the boil, reduce heat and simmer, covered, for 15 minutes.
2. Melt butter in another large pan; add onion, pepper, celery and garlic and cook slowly 20 minutes or until very tender.
3. Add okra and tomato mixture to vegetables; add tomato paste, peppers, thyme, oregano, bay leaves, allspice, chilli, sauce and stock. Bring to the boil, reduce heat and simmer, uncovered, 15 minutes.

NOTE: This dish can be eaten immediately or frozen in serving portions. Add prawns, chicken, ham, beetroot or other vegetables. Serve with rice.

PICKLED ONIONS

1kg (2 1/4lb) baby onions

225g (8oz) salt

2 litres (3 1/2 pints) water

100g (4oz) sugar

6 black peppercorns

6 whole cloves

cinnamon stick

4 blades mace (optional)

2 teaspoons whole allspice

500ml (18fl oz) white wine vinegar

red chillies, for bottling

1. Peel onions and place in large bowl; add salt and water and stir well. Cover and allow to stand 2 days, stirring occasionally.
2. Combine sugar, peppercorns, spices and vinegar in a large pan. Add drained onions; stir over low heat until sugar dissolves. Bring to boil, remove from heat and stand 1 hour. Remove onions with a slotted spoon; strain spiced vinegar and reserve liquid.
3. Pack drained onions into warm, sterilised jars, including 2–3 chillies in each jar. Pour vinegar over onions and chillies and seal.

NOTE: Store onions in cool dark place for up to a year. Refrigerate after opening.

PARSNIP CHUTNEY

1kg (2 1/4lb) parsnips

3 onions

1 orange

350ml (12fl oz) vinegar

250ml (8fl oz) water

250g (9oz) soft brown sugar

250g (9oz) dates

1 tablespoon curry powder

1/2 teaspoon garam masala

2 teaspoons salt

1. Peel and finely chop parsnips and onions. Peel orange and shred peel thinly; chop flesh coarsely.
2. Place parsnips, onions, orange rind, vinegar and water in large pan. Bring to boil, reduce heat and simmer, uncovered, 1 hour. Add sugar, dates, curry powder, garam masala and salt; stir over medium heat until sugar dissolves. Bring to boil, reduce heat and simmer, uncovered, until mixture thickens, stirring occasionally.
3. Remove from heat and stand 5 minutes before spooning into warm, sterilised jars; seal.

NOTE: Store for up to six months. Refrigerate after opening. Serve with chicken or beef curry.

PUMPKIN JAM

250g (9oz) dried apricots, chopped

1 litre (1 3/4 pints) water

500g (1lb 2oz) pumpkin, peeled and chopped

100ml (4fl oz) orange juice

1 tablespoon chopped glacé ginger

1 tablespoon chopped crystallised pawpaw

900g (2lb) sugar

1. Combine apricots and water in bowl; cover and allow to stand overnight.
2. Combine apricots and water, pumpkin, juice, ginger and pawpaw in large pan. Bring to boil, reduce heat and simmer, covered, 20 minutes or until pumpkin is soft. Add sugar, stirring constantly until dissolved. Bring to boil; boil, without stirring, 30 minutes or until jam is thick and falls heavily from a wooden spoon.
3. Spoon into warm, sterilised jars; seal.

NOTE: Store jam up to 2 months in refrigerator.

RADISH TZATZIKI

20 radishes

350ml (12 fl oz) plain yoghurt

2 tablespoons lemon juice

salt and pepper, to taste

1. Wash and grate radishes.
2. Combine yoghurt and lemon juice in bowl; add radish. Mix well, season to taste. Cover and allow to stand 5 minutes before serving.

NOTE: Serve as a dip or with roast lamb. Can be stored for up to a day in refrigerator.

SWEETCORN RELISH

8 sweetcorn cobs

2 red peppers

2 green peppers

2 medium onions, finely chopped

8 celery stalks, finely chopped

1.5 litres (2 1/2 pints) cider vinegar

100g (4oz) sugar

3 tablespoons mustard seeds

3 teaspoons salt

4 allspice berries

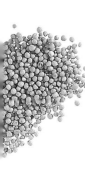

1. Remove and discard husks and silks from corn. Slice kernels from each cob. Remove and discard seeds and membranes from peppers; chop finely.
2. Combine sweetcorn kernels, peppers, onions, celery, vinegar, sugar, seeds, salt and berries in large pan. Stir over low heat until sugar has dissolved.
3. Bring mixture to boil, reduce heat and simmer 15–20 minutes or until vegetables are tender, stirring occasionally. Spoon into warm, sterilised jars and seal.

NOTE: Store sweetcorn relish for several months in a cool, dry place. Refrigerate after

opening. Serve on cheese sandwiches or combine with mayonnaise and serve with poached eggs.

TOMATO PASTE

5kg (11lb) ripe tomatoes

1 tablespoon salt

white pepper, to taste

olive oil

1. Chop tomatoes roughly and place in large pan. Cook over medium heat 20–25 minutes or until very soft, stirring occasionally. Remove from heat.
2. Place tomatoes in food processor and process 30 seconds or until puréed. Return to pan and bring to boil; reduce heat and simmer, uncovered, until the mixture is reduced by half. Preheat the oven to very low, 120°C (240–250°F, gas mark 1/2).
3. Transfer the puréed tomatoes to a greased baking dish and bake 4–5 hours or until paste is very thick and concentrated. Add salt and pepper and spoon into warm, sterilised jars. Cover with a thin layer of olive oil and seal.

NOTE: Tomato paste will keep for up to a year in a cool, dry place. Because it is used so often, this is an ideal recipe if you have a glut of tomatoes which are on the verge of becoming over-ripe.

TOMATO SAUCE

2kg (4 1/2lb) ripe tomatoes, roughly chopped

4 medium brown onions, finely chopped

2 cloves garlic, roughly chopped

1 tablespoon salt

1 tablespoon black pepper

1/2 teaspoon cayenne pepper

6 whole cloves

350g (12oz) soft brown sugar

450ml (3/4 pint) white wine vinegar

1. Combine tomatoes, onions, garlic, salt, peppers and cloves in a large heavy-based pan. Cook gently over medium heat for 45 minutes or until soft.
2. Add sugar and vinegar and continue to cook over low heat until mixture thickens to sauce consistency.
3. Strain mixture through a sieve and pour into warm sterilised jars and seal.

NOTE: Leave for 2 weeks before using. Store in a cool, dry place.

SPICY BARBECUE SAUCE

2 large red peppers, seeds and
 membrane removed, rough chopped
2kg (4^1/2lb) ripe tomatoes, rough chopped
3 medium onions, finely chopped
3 sticks celery, finely chopped
600ml (1 pint) malt vinegar
2 red chillies, finely chopped
3 cloves garlic, crushed
2 teaspoons grated fresh ginger
1 tablespoon fresh coriander leaves,
 shredded
1 teaspoon ground cumin
1 teaspoon mixed spice
2 teaspoons ground black pepper
1 teaspoon hot English mustard
2 tablespoons paprika
1 teaspoon Tabasco
250g (9oz) soft brown sugar

1. Combine peppers, tomatoes, onions, celery, vinegar, chillies, garlic, ginger, coriander, cumin, spice, pepper, mustard, paprika and Tabasco in a large heavy-based pan. Bring to boil, stirring occasionally over medium heat. Reduce heat, simmer uncovered for 1 hour.
2. Cool slightly for about 15 minutes, pour into food processor and purée. Return mixture to pan. Add sugar and stir over low heat until sugar is dissolved. Simmer for 30 minutes or until mixture is thick enough to coat the back of a spoon.
3. Pour mixture into hot sterilised jars; seal immediately. Leave 2 days before using.

GREEN TOMATO CHUTNEY

1.5kg (3^1/4lb) green tomatoes, chopped
2 small green apples, peeled and chopped
1 large onion, chopped
1 teaspoon salt
75g (3oz) sultanas
1 teaspoon whole black peppercorns
1 tablespoon brown mustard seeds
350g (12oz) soft brown sugar
450ml (3/4 pint) white vinegar
^{1}/2 teaspoon sweet paprika

1. Place all ingredients in a large, heavy-based pan. Stir over low heat until sugar dissolves.
2. Increase heat to medium and bring mixture to the boil. Simmer, uncovered, for 1–1^1/2 hours, or until chutney has thickened. Stir mixture occasionally. Stir more frequently towards the end of cooking time to ensure mixture does not catch or burn.
3. Remove from heat, set aside for 5 minutes. Pour mixture into hot, sterilised jars; seal immediately. Label and date when cool. Store in a cool, dark place for up to 12 months.

TOMATO CHILLI JAM

2 large red peppers
4 red chillies, finely chopped
2kg (4^1/2lb) tomatoes, peeled and chopped
4 green apples, peeled and grated
4 garlic cloves, crushed
1 tablespoon finely grated lemon rind
175ml (6fl oz) lemon juice
800g (1^3/4lb) sugar

1. Cut peppers into large pieces and remove seeds and membrane. Place on a baking tray and cook under a hot grill 5 minutes or until skin is completely blackened. Remove from heat; cover with a clean damp tea-towel and cool completely. Peel skin from peppers and chop flesh finely.
2. Place peppers, chillies, tomatoes, apples, garlic and lemon rind in a large pan. Bring to the boil, reduce heat and simmer 20 minutes.
3. Add lemon juice and sugar to pan. Stir until sugar has dissolved. Simmer 1 hour, stirring occasionally.
4. Remove jam from heat and allow to stand 5 minutes. Spoon jam into warm, sterilised jars and seal.

NOTE: Store for up to a year.

TO SUN-DRY TOMATOES

Choose firm, ripe plum tomatoes. Plunge tomatoes into boiling water, remove immediately and plunge into cold water; drain and dry. Cut tomatoes in half lengthways. Line racks or deep trays with double layers of muslin. Arrange tomatoes, cut-side up, on racks and place racks outdoors, leaving room underneath for circulation. (Cover with netting to protect tomatoes from insects, if you like.) Tomatoes will take about 3–5 days to dry out, depending on the weather. Bring tomatoes in during cool nights or periods of humidity. Turn tomatoes over when you can see that the moisture on one side has completely evaporated. Tomatoes are ready when they have a chewy, slightly leathery texture. Loosely pack in plastic bags or glass jars and store for 5–7 days before using, shaking occasionally. Store firmly packed in oil in glass containers. Use within a year.

TO OVEN-DRY TOMATOES

Preheat oven to very slow 80°C (175°F, lowest setting). Place prepared tomatoes cut-side up on wire racks in baking trays and place in oven. Leave oven door open slightly and turn on the oven-fan if you have one. Tomatoes will take up to 16 hours to dry. Turn trays frequently and remove pieces as they are done. Apart from their usual uses in sandwiches and on antipasto platters, these tomatoes can also be used in slow-cooking dishes such as casseroles.

TURNIP PICKLE

2 small beetroot

1kg (2¼lb) turnips, peeled

1 litre (1¾ pints) white wine vinegar

2–4 tablespoons sugar

2 small chillies

2 bay leaves

2 tablespoons coriander seeds

1. Scrub beetroot thoroughly, dry and chop finely. Slice turnips thinly.
2. Combine vinegar and sugar in large pan; stir over medium heat until sugar dissolves. Cool.
3. Pack turnip slices, beetroot, chillies, bay leaves and coriander seeds into warm, sterilised jars; cover with vinegar mixture and seal.

NOTE: Store in a cool, dark place 5 days before use. Store for 3 months in refrigerator.

COURGETTE CHUTNEY

1.5kg (3¼lb) plums

500g (1lb 2oz) courgettes, finely chopped

500g (1lb 2oz) onions, finely chopped

250g (9oz) sultanas

675g (1½lb) soft brown sugar

2 teaspoons ground ginger

1 teaspoon dry mustard

1 litre (1¾ pints) malt vinegar

1. Wash, stone and chop plums coarsely.
2. Combine plums, courgettes, onions, sugar, sultanas, ginger, mustard and 500ml (18fl oz) vinegar in large pan. Stir over medium heat until sugar dissolves; reduce heat and simmer, uncovered, 30 minutes. Add remaining vinegar and simmer 2 hours, stirring occasionally, until mixture is thick.
3. Spoon into warm, sterilised jars and seal.

NOTE: Store 1 month before using. Store for up to a year in a cool, dry place.

COURGETTE PICKLE

1.5kg (3¼lb) courgettes

450g (1lb) onions

225g (8oz) salt

2.5 litres (4½ pints) water

1 litre (1¾ pints) white wine vinegar

225g (8oz) sugar

2 teaspoons mustard seeds

1 tablespoon celery seeds

1 tablespoon allspice berries

1. Slice courgettes thinly. Peel onions and slice thinly. Combine salt and water in a large bowl; add courgettes and onions and leave to stand 3 hours, stirring occasionally. Rinse in cold water, drain well and dry on paper towels.
2. Combine vinegar, sugar, seeds and berries in pan; stir over medium heat until sugar dissolves. Remove from heat, add courgettes and onions and leave to stand 1 hour.
3. Return pan to heat; bring to boil. Boil 3 minutes and remove from heat. Spoon mixture into warm, sterilised jars and seal.

NOTE: Store for 2 weeks before serving. Will keep for up to a year in a cool, dry place.

VEGETABLE STOCK

2 carrots

2 stalks celery, tops left on

1 whole leek

2 tomatoes

1 onion

10 sprigs flat-leaf parsley

15g (½ oz) butter

1 tablespoon olive oil

1 bay leaf

2–3 black peppercorns

1 tablespoon grated lemon rind

1.2 litres (2 pints) water

1. Coarsely chop vegetables and parsley.
2. Melt butter and oil in large pan; add vegetables and stir over medium heat 3–5 minutes or until soft. Add bay leaf, peppercorns, lemon rind and water.
3. Bring stock to boil, reduce heat and simmer, covered, 1 hour. Cool and strain.

NOTE: Stock can be refrigerated for up to 3 days or frozen up to 6 months. A good idea is to freeze stock in ice-cube trays – stock can then be used in small portions as needed. Use any combination of vegetables for this basic stock.

INDEX

Published by Merehurst Limited, 1998
Ferry House, 51-57 Lacy Road, Putney, London SW15 1PR

Text copyright © Merehurst Limited
Photography copyright © Murdoch Books (except those listed below)

ISBN S405/1-85391-699-4

SERIES EDITOR: Graham Strong

EDITOR: John Negus

TEXT: John Fenton-Smith

DESIGNER: Karen Awadzi

CREATIVE DIRECTOR: Marylouise Brammer

MANAGING EDITOR: Christine Eslick

COMMISSIONING EDITOR: Helen Griffin

PUBLISHER: Anne Wilson

PHOTOGRAPHS: All photographs by Lorna Rose except those by
Denise Greig pp 10 (L and R), 29, 64 (L);
Stirling Macoboy p 48; Reg Morrison pp 46-47, 50, 53 (R), 54, 56-57, 70;
Joe Filshie p 66; Graham Strong pp 21, 25 mini, 34 mini, 37, 38 mini, 60 mini;
Michael Warren pp 13, 19, 34, 62; Thompson & Morgan p 69 (L);
Eric Sawford p 62; Suttons pp 25, 26; Mr Fothergill's pp 7, 14, 60, 61 mini; Marshalls p 51;
Unwins pp 24, 38, 44, 61(R); Pat Brindley pp 6, 14 (L), 15 (L), 61(R);
and John Negus pp 7 (L), 15(R), 31.

FRONT COVER: A brilliant collection of tomatoes
TITLE PAGE: Young courgettes with flowers attached